Get Rid *of* the Mess

Decluttering What You Don't Need
to Make Space for What Matters Most

Jenna Ford

Copyright 2023 © Calm Waters Publishing House

All rights reserved.
The contents of this book may not be reproduced, duplicated or transmitted without direct written permission from the author.

Under no circumstances will any legal responsibility or blame be held against the publisher for any reparation, damages, or monetary loss due to the information herein, either directly or indirectly.

Interior layout and design by Davor Nikolic

Legal Notice:
This book is copyright protected. This is only for personal use. You cannot amend, distribute, sell, use, quote or paraphrase any part or the content within this book without the consent of the author.

Disclaimer Notice:
Please note the information contained within this document is for educational and entertainment purposes only. Every attempt has been made to provide accurate, up to date and reliable complete information. No warranties of any kind are expressed or implied. Readers acknowledge that the author is not engaging in the rendering of legal, financial, medical or professional advice. The content of this book has been derived from various sources. Please consult a licensed professional before attempting any techniques outlined in this book.
By reading this document, the reader agrees that under no circumstances is the author responsible for any losses, direct or indirect, which are incurred as a result of the use of information contained within this document, including, but not limited to, —errors, omissions, or inaccuracies.

Contents

Introduction	1
CHAPTER 1: The Clutter Cycle	7
What is the Clutter Cycle?	7
How You Contribute to the Clutter Cycle	9
The Impact of Clutter on Physical Health	12
The Impact of Clutter on Mental Health	13
The Clutter Cycle Run Amok	15
Key Takeaways from Chapter 1	15
CHAPTER 2: What's Your Why?	17
How to Craft Your Meaningful Why	18
Transforming Your Initial Why into a More Meaningful Why	21
Key Takeaways from Chapter 2	23
CHAPTER 3: The Past and the Future	25
How Did All This Clutter Get Here?	25
Where Is Your Home on the Clutter Scale?	30
Visualize It so You Can Achieve It	33
Key Takeaways from Chapter 3	34
CHAPTER 4: Setting the Stage for Success	35
3 Steps to Set Yourself Up for Success	36
Write Down Your Plan	37
Creating Your Plan	37
Time Block	40
Key Takeaways from Chapter 4	44
CHAPTER 5: It's Time to Declutter!	45
The Ultimate Guide to a Tidy Home	47
Sorting Tips	50
Analysis Paralysis	52
Five Essential Questions	52
Keeping Items	56
Recycling and Responsibly Disposing of Items	56
Donating Items	57
Giving Away Items	58

Selling Items	58
Moving Forward	60
Key Lessons from Chapter 5	61
CHAPTER 6: Finding Motivation	**67**
Motivation Tips & Tricks	70
See the Possibilities	71
Key Lessons From Chapter 6	73
CHAPTER 7: Working through Roadblocks and Maintaining Momentum	**75**
Common Roadblocks	78
What Ifs	82
Scarcity Mindset	83
Sentimental Feelings	85
Walking through Roadblocks	86
Other Underlying Challenges	95
Key Lessons from Chapter 7	97
CHAPTER 8: Engaging Others in Your Plan and Getting Help	**99**
The Big Discussion	100
General Guidelines for Involving Children	102
Working Together	104
Resistance from Your Partner or Spouse	105
Hiring a Professional	106
Moving Forward	108
Key Lessons From Chapter 8	108
CHAPTER 9: Organizing Systems That Work	**109**
Organizational Tools	110
Organizational Principles	111
Organizational Hacks by Room	112
Organizational Tips and Tricks	114
Key Lessons From Chapter 9	116
CHAPTER 10: Maintaining Long-Term Success	**117**
Control What Comes In	119
Key Lessons From Chapter 10	121
Conclusion	123
Bibliography	127

Introduction

> *"The biggest adventure you can ever take is to live the life of your dreams."*
>
> —Oprah Winfrey

You never know what happens behind closed doors. So here's a snippet of my story to show you what happened behind mine.

No one's life is perfect, but I was dealt a pretty good hand. It's been an incredible journey so far, and I'm grateful for that. I'm a happy working mom of two girls, with a supportive husband and two tiny dogs. Within six years, my husband and I got engaged and then married, moved twice, remodeled our home, had two children (one after the other), and managed careers that were in full swing and included travel, long hours, and plenty of stress. Mind you, we got married "later" in life, and I was no longer in my twenties, or even thirties. I was often totally exhausted and eventually found myself on the edge of burnout.

With my life as it was, I let things pile up around the home for a few years. The girls grew quickly, moving from one size of clothing to the next, and they had more toys than I could have ever dreamed of as a child. Then COVID turned life upside down, and a new layer of clutter built up as we worked, played, and "went to" school, all at home. By this point, I had shifted the focus of my work and had more time for my family and other priorities, but I still lacked the energy and the will to dig us out of the mess we had created.

Ugh. I hated it. I loved my family but hated our home full of clutter — and worse, I felt responsible. The mess was a dark cloud hanging over my head, and it was holding me back from doing more with my life. I wanted to feel relaxed and happy in my home. I wanted to focus on my work without being distracted by all the stuff around me. I wanted to invite friends over without the need for a manic, all-night cleaning session. I wanted to quickly find what I needed without a frustrating wild goose chase. I wanted to be present with my family without constantly feeling that I should be cleaning instead. I wanted to create memories with my family, and I wanted my girls to remember me as more than the mom who wanted a clean house.

I fantasized about cleaning out my closet and told myself I was going to do it more times than I'd like to admit, but I never did. I binge-watched just about every home decluttering and organizing show, and they sometimes catapulted me into small spurts of decluttering, but I never quite finished what I started. Conveniently (or inconveniently), I experienced my strongest motivational moments when it was impossible to get to work on the clutter — like when I was driving, in the shower, at a soccer game, or when it was already way past my bedtime. The desire was there, but I was overwhelmed and just didn't want to shackle myself to our home and spend my life trying to dig us out of the mess we'd created.

How did my friends' homes look so pulled together all the time? Was it because they had more space than us? No. I knew that even if we had a garage, it would eventually become yet another dumping ground for unsorted items. More space wasn't the answer. So, what contributed to my tendency to accumulate stuff?

Well, I'm creative and analytical, a creator, a dreamer, and a doer with multiple projects going on at all times. I have a strong sentimental core. I'm also a former self-proclaimed workaholic with perfectionist tendencies and a splash of adult ADHD. While this quirky cocktail of qualities creates a unique me and comes with plenty of positives, I also accept that together, these qualities likely enable the "perfect storm" and contribute to my tendency to collect things. I call myself "clutter-challenged."

On the flip side, I've always embraced self-improvement and have plenty of experience creating order out of chaos, so when I finally came to terms with how much the clutter in our home was holding me back, I changed. It seems obvious in hindsight, but I finally realized that getting our clutter under control was a form of self-care. I realized that I had to prioritize what used to seem like a daunting and tedious activity because not doing so had real-life consequences that went well beyond appearances.

This book will share my decluttering strategies with you — and they work! Through my own metamorphosis, I have become passionate about the transformative power of decluttering and wanted to help others along the way. This book will help you triumph over the clutter in your home — and in your mind — and help you live the life you were meant to live. It's easy to put off decluttering, but making it a focus and working through it is well worth the effort. Decluttering can lift your spirits, help you take charge of your life, and convert a chaotic living environment into a warm and welcoming home with all the space — both physical and mental — you need to thrive.

As I decluttered our home, my stress faded, and I felt an amazing sense of freedom. The dark cloud hanging over my head drifted away, and I could focus on the things that mattered in my life — being there for my family and friends, working out, focusing on my well-being, creating new experiences, and my career. Living in a decluttered home was a breath of fresh air.

Before continuing, let's get on the same page about decluttering. You don't have to organize or clean in connection with it. Yes, there's a connection between decluttering, organizing, and cleaning, but they're not the same thing. Decluttering means getting rid of things you aren't using and don't really need anymore. It's a simple activity, but it's not always easy. And while this book will touch on organizing and cleaning, its primary focus is decluttering.

The fantastic thing about my decluttering process is that you can start out small, taking it one drawer, one tabletop, or one closet at a time. As you move through your home, sorting through everything and setting aside what you decide not to keep, you get one step closer to the day you can banish clutter from your life for good.

So, what are the benefits of decluttering? Some of the most exciting include:

- **Personal empowerment.** When you declutter, you'll feel accomplished. Afterward, you can either sit back and put your feet up or move on to the next thing on your to-do list, filled with renewed self-confidence.
- **Home beautification and more space.** Your home will look cleaner, fresher, and more spacious when you scale down what you own. You will have a clean slate for years to come.
- **Greater peace of mind.** Living in an uncluttered environment can reduce your anxiety. Your home will become a tranquil oasis for you and your family.
- **Improved physical health.** Clutter produces and attracts dust and other unhealthy airborne particles, which affect your health and lower the quality of your living space. With the clutter — and allergens — gone, you should be able to breathe easy once again.
- **Family togetherness.** When you declutter your home as a family, it will be something you can celebrate together.
- **Time to spend on what matters.** When you get your clutter under control, you won't waste time looking for things or trying to organize stuff that you have too

much of. You'll reclaim time to spend on what's really important to you.

You may be familiar with the concept of decluttering. Perhaps you've tried to declutter your home already but gave up because you got overwhelmed. Or maybe you felt like you didn't have the time to get it done right. This doesn't mean you lack the willpower or the skills to tackle the job. Maybe you couldn't garner motivation yet. Or perhaps you needed more tools or a plan to keep you on track.

This book will help you with that. Not only will you learn more about the empowering potential of decluttering, but you will also gain tools to help you overcome roadblocks and obstacles that may have prevented you from getting through the job in the past. I will also help you develop a plan of action with manageable steps and achievable milestones, both of which are essential for your short- and long-term success.

It's important to recognize that clutter does not mean you are personally flawed, wasteful, or extravagant. We all have strengths and challenges, and life gets crazy sometimes. Much of what you accumulated likely had meaning at some point. Much of it reflects the joys and memories from the past. However, when you let go of things, you can live a more fulfilling life in the present.

As you read through this book, here are a few pieces of advice to follow:

- Keep an open mind and try the exercises. They will help you overcome hurdles common to the decluttering process.
- Work through the book step by step, but feel free to change things if something doesn't work for you or might work better with a tweak.
- Recognize and accept that clutter doesn't mean you're inadequate or "less than" as a person. Clutter happens,

and while it seems like it should be simple to fix, that's not always the case. Although you may have allowed a little (or a mountain of) clutter to build up, it doesn't reflect who you are as a person.
- Remember that with a little commitment and a change of habits, you can control clutter in the future.

This book was written to help you change your life. When you feel confident about beginning to declutter, start! Pick up the book again when you get stuck or need help maintaining motivation. Whether you need to ramp up your motivation, overcome hurdles, shift your mindset, or get specific tips on how to go about decluttering in a way that will help you make real progress, you can find guidance in the chapters ahead.

When you begin to declutter and make room for what matters the most, you'll finally have space to live, move, and breathe. Change might take some time, but it will make all the difference.

I'm excited for you! If I could do it, so can you.

Let's get started.

CHAPTER 1:

The Clutter Cycle

*"Clutter isn't just the stuff in your closet;
it's anything that gets between you and
the life that you want to be living."*

– Peter Walsh

Clutter. It surrounds you. How did it get here? How did it get to this point?

Life is busy. Things often fly under the radar, and before you know it, clutter is staring you in the face. Let's take a look at how clutter enters your home and takes up residence.

What is the Clutter Cycle?

Clutter builds up over time. It starts from the smallest beginnings and then spreads across your entire living space, invading every nook and cranny of your home.

How does the clutter cycle begin and build up?
1. Allowing items to enter the home: From last-minute purchases to buying duplicates or receiving gifts, things come into your home and accumulate. This has even more of an impact if you don't have space to store what you bring in. Soon, you have an unnecessary surplus of stuff.

2. A lack of space or designated places for items: When things don't have a specific place, it's easy to lose them in the back of closets or at the bottom of piles, and it's less painful to buy replacement items than to find what you already own.
3. No organization or desire to organize: When items aren't managed well, they become useless, obsolete, broken, or unwanted.
4. Disposal: Sometimes things get tossed, and other times, they don't. People sometimes grab a large garbage bag and fill it and think that that's the extent of decluttering. Unfortunately, it takes a little more thought and effort than that.

The clutter cycle is circular, and once you slip into it, you're like a hamster trapped on its wheel, running in place but never going anywhere. The cycle is aggravated when stress, fatigue, and overwhelm take over — and stress shopping only adds to the problem. Like other cycles, the clutter cycle will repeat itself until you understand how it operates.

Clutter doesn't accumulate randomly. The extra clothes, mementos, worn-out shoes, broken sports gear, outdated cable TV equipment, empty boxes or bottles, toys your children no longer play with — all the things you've been holding on to unnecessarily — were brought into your home for a reason but didn't leave your home when you were done with them.

Once you learn more about the nature of clutter and reflect on your situation, you should build an awareness of how your clutter accumulated. But until then, the cycle will remain unbroken, even if you manage to remove some of the stuff and spruce up your home from time to time.

CHAPTER 1:

How You Contribute to the Clutter Cycle

No one sets out to gather more things than they need. Despite living functional, well-adjusted lives for the most part, many people just can't control their accumulation of household goods.

If your home is overflowing with stuff, and clutter has gotten the upper hand, there are some possible explanations.

Lifestyle Challenges

Many people work long hours, including nights and weekends. Sometimes it's driven by economic necessity, and in other cases, it's motivated by workaholic tendencies. When free time becomes available, you most likely won't be eager to spend a Saturday afternoon rummaging through your home looking for things to take to Goodwill.

There are also family and personal responsibilities to consider. Maybe you have school-age children who need your attention, a partner or significant other you want to spend time with, a dating life, or older parents and relatives who need special care and assistance. All of these can mean a very full schedule, and if you haven't prioritized decluttering in the past, it's an easy thing to put to the side now.

But unfortunately, if you don't make time to declutter, your clutter will make plenty of time for you.

Life Stage Changes

As you move through the various stages of your life, even the slightest tendency to hold onto things for too long can snowball into a problem.

As your life moves from one stage to the next, it sometimes becomes more complex and may include expanding or changing family situations. Plus, the more time you spend on earth, the more opportunity you'll have to collect things. And when stuff comes in and never goes out, clutter builds up.

Getting older won't make you more tolerant of clutter, but it can definitely sap you of the energy you need to purge the excess. This is especially true if you have health conditions that affect your mobility, energy, or activity level.

Psychological Factors

If you struggle with procrastination, you're not alone. In a recent survey, approximately 50 percent of adults admitted to procrastinating on occasion, and 20 to 25 percent said they did so chronically.[1] When asked why they procrastinate, the top reasons were task aversion (meaning the task was perceived as intimidating or unpleasant), low energy, fear of failure, and a lack of self-confidence.

When decluttering seems daunting, procrastination often takes over. In addition, feelings of guilt, shame, embarrassment, and frustration can sap your motivation. But delaying dealing with your extra stuff will only make things worse. Breaking the clutter cycle once and for all will happen when you put aside your negative self-judgments and replace them with determination to succeed.

If you feel ashamed of your clutter and blame yourself for not dealing with it sooner, I get it. Let's work through your emotions and how to declutter together.

---

[1] Sam David, 'Fascinating Statistics On Procrastination (Based On Research and Surveys)', *Proactivity Lab* (blog), 3 January 2023, https://proactivitylab.com/fascinating-statistics-on-procrastination-based-on-research-and-surveys/.

CHAPTER 1:

Emotional Attachments

Psychological factors, lifestyle changes, and life stage changes all contribute to and reinforce the clutter cycle. But a big factor that leaves you vulnerable to cluttering your home is your emotional attachment.

Keepsakes and mementos come in all shapes and forms. To some degree, most of us are sentimental about things that remind us of our successes, parents or relatives who are no longer with us, and special moments in our past. If you have children, you've probably saved many things that remind you of their milestones.

Sentiment and nostalgia are the culprits for a lot of the clutter in some people's homes. Having treasured keepsakes around you can be comforting, even if you have no use for them or don't even look at them anymore. Throwing away items attached to memories or people can feel wrong, but remember that you will always have your memories of the good times and the people in your past — and those matter much more than things.

Getting past these feelings might be one of the most challenging things you have to do when you start decluttering. But once you begin to say goodbye to items from your past, you'll find out that it's not as difficult as you think — and then you can start living in the present.

Take a moment to think about and note what led you to accumulate clutter. Remember this as you work through the different exercises in this book.

_____

_____

_____

_____

The Impact of Clutter on Physical Health

Clutter affects your physical and mental health. And as the clutter cycle continues, so do the adverse effects on your health.

Cluttered environments are dusty ones. Most physical objects decay over time, and when you have a lot of things, your home can quickly fill up with the dust that all this crumbling and disintegrating creates.

In addition to the dust the clutter itself makes, clutter increases the surfaces for dust and other pollutants to cling to. Cleaning everything in a home filled with things is time-consuming and virtually impossible. And it's not just an issue of aesthetics. Indoor air pollution caused by clutter can have consequences for your health. Many studies have linked indoor exposure to dust and other pollutants to breathing problems, asthma, skin and respiratory allergies, and an increased vulnerability to colds and the flu.[2]

In one alarming meta-study published in 2015, scientists from several research institutions looked at the data from tests of indoor air quality in homes in the United States. They found forty-five proven toxic chemicals contaminating a significant number of homes, and ten of these chemicals were found in over 90 percent of the samples tested.[3] These chemicals are hidden in plastics, personal care products, cleaning products, carpeting, decaying paper, electronic devices, and cookware.

Obesity is another potential negative consequence of clutter. A 2015 study revealed a direct link between the collection of clutter and body mass index (BMI), as people who lived in

---

[2] Sotiris Vardoulakis et al., 'Indoor Exposure to Selected Air Pollutants in the Home Environment: A Systematic Review', *International Journal of Environmental Research and Public Health* 17, no. 23 (December 2020): 8972, https://doi.org/10.3390/ijerph17238972.

[3] Veena Singla, 'Not Just Dirt: Toxic Chemicals in Indoor Dust', Issue Brief, NRDC, 14 September 2016, https://www.nrdc.org/resources/not-just-dirt-toxic-chemicals-indoor-dust.

severely cluttered homes were 77 percent more likely to be overweight.[4] Another study published in 2016 found that college students living in residences with messy kitchen environments were more likely to experience stressful feelings leading to compulsive consumption of junk food than students exposed to orderly kitchens.[5]

Clutter can make you unhealthy, especially if you live in a cluttered environment for an extended period. When you break the cycle, you can also help break the cycle of poor health.

The Impact of Clutter on Mental Health

Clutter takes a toll on your mental health. When your home is disorganized, and you're surrounded by objects strewn haphazardly about, it affects your psychological and emotional well-being. Your brain constantly thinks that your work isn't done, and it won't rest until you clear out the mess — the chaos and sensory overload can make it impossible to relax. This is a huge one for me.

Another clutter issue is that it's distracting and makes it difficult to focus or concentrate. This can be a concern if you work from home, as many of us do nowadays. Clutter and a lack of order and organization also interfere with your cognitive processes — learning and remembering are more difficult, creativity is suppressed, and analytical and logical thinking is hindered.

These assertions aren't based exclusively on anecdotal evidence. Many studies have shown how clutter can compromise your mental health, and more are being published every year.

---

[4] Amanda M. Raines et al., 'Hoarding and Eating Pathology: The Mediating Role of Emotion Regulation', *Comprehensive Psychiatry* 57 (February 2015): 29–35, https://doi.org/10.1016/j.comppsych.2014.11.005.
[5] Lenny R. Vartanian, Kristin M. Kernan, and Brian Wansink, 'Clutter, Chaos, and Overconsumption: The Role of Mind-Set in Stressful and Chaotic Food Environments', *Environment and Behavior* 49, no. 2 (1 February 2017): 215–23, https://doi.org/10.1177/0013916516628178.

For example:
- A study carried out at UCLA in 2012 found that living in a home with a high density of household objects elevated cortisol, the hormone responsible for generating feelings of stress. In the same study, researchers found that living in clutter can cause depression, a loss of self-esteem, and feelings of shame and inadequacy.[6]
- In a 2016 study published in the *Journal of Environmental Psychology,* researchers surveyed adult residents of the United States and Canada to learn about their experiences with clutter. Those who admitted to living in a cluttered home environment reported an increase in stress, a decrease in productivity, and negative feelings about their overall well-being.[7]
- A 2016 study discussed in the Proceedings of the National Academy of Sciences (PNAS) found that visual distractions caused by clutter inhibited working memory and restricted cognitive activity in general.[8]

Conversely, many studies have shown that decluttering brings some enormous mental health benefits by reversing the side effects of living in a cluttered environment.

---

[6] Closet Factory, 'UCLA Study Finds Stress Caused by Clutter', Closet Factory, 11 September 2017, https://www.closetfactory.com/blog/ucla-study-finds-stress-caused-by-clutter/.

[7] Catherine A. Roster, Joseph R. Ferrari, and M. Peter Jurkat, 'The Dark Side of Home: Assessing Possession "Clutter" on Subjective Well-Being', Journal of Environmental Psychology 46 (1 June 2016): 32–41, https://doi.org/10.1016/j.jenvp.2016.03.003.

[8] John M. Gaspar et al., 'Inability to Suppress Salient Distractors Predicts Low Visual Working Memory Capacity', Proceedings of the National Academy of Sciences 113, no. 13 (29 March 2016): 3693–98, https://doi.org/10.1073/pnas.1523471113.

CHAPTER 1:

The Clutter Cycle Run Amok

One of the hard and fast rules of the clutter cycle is that clutter begets clutter. When you don't learn how to declutter effectively and don't act on it, the clutter will continue to accumulate.

The good news is that you don't have to be a prisoner to clutter forever because decluttering begets decluttering. Once you've developed a rhythm of effective strategies for sustainable decluttering, backed by the proper mindset and habits, you'll be able to break the clutter cycle once and for all.

KEY TAKEAWAYS FROM CHAPTER 1

- Clutter takes on a life of its own, and that's why you have to break the cycle before you can declutter for good.
- Possessions accumulate because of lifestyle changes, life stage changes, psychological factors, and sentimental attachments.
- Dust and other contaminants generated by and attracted by clutter can have a negative effect on your physical health.
- Being surrounded by too many objects and too much chaos can cause stress, anxiety, depression, insomnia, and other mental and behavioral health issues.
- Clutter begets clutter; however, when using the right strategies and learning how to overcome your roadblocks, decluttering begets decluttering.

CHAPTER 2:

What's Your Why?

*"When your why is big enough,
you will find your how."*

– Les Brown

Your decluttering project needs a powerful *why*. When you know why you are embarking on a decluttering journey, your chances of success rise substantially.

It was only when I found my *why* that I was able to reach my decluttering goals. Your *why* is your reason for undertaking a challenge — and it's the reason you'll see that challenge through to the end, no matter what obstacles or roadblocks stand in your way.

Each person has their unique *why*. It's the spark that drives you and keeps you going, especially on days when the tasks at hand get too overwhelming or you just feel like giving up. Motivation alone will fail you unless you find a *why* that's so deeply rooted in what's important to you that nothing will stand in your way.

If you continue along the same path you've been on, your clutter-free future may never come. Finding your *why* before you start decluttering can lay the groundwork for change to come. A compelling *why* will get you up and moving and keep you pushing forward until you've achieved your decluttering goal.

How to Craft Your Meaningful Why

Your *why* spells out your motivation for decluttering and connects it with a sense of purpose. It becomes your truth when you write it down. Your statement should be one or two sentences long and include an action and an impact.

For example, "To (action) so that (impact)".

Example: "I want to *declutter my home* so that *I can be less stressed and be a better version of myself, both for my family and my own happiness.* This will help me live my best life."

Here are a few questions you can ask yourself to help you create your *why*:
1. What would your life look or feel like if your home was free of clutter?
2. What would change in your life (and your family members' lives) if your home had less stuff?
3. What do you hope decluttering will do for you (and your family)?
4. What inspires you to declutter your home?

If you need more help capturing your authentic *why*, reviewing some of the benefits of decluttering can help. There are wonderful perks that come with having a decluttered home!

Less stress and anxiety and more happiness

In 2010, a study published in the *Journal of Personality and Social Psychology* looked at the impact of clutter on Los Angeles-area married couples with dual incomes and at least one school-age child — and the study hit close to home. It found that women, in particular, experienced elevated levels of the stress hormone cortisol when living in cluttered environments.[1] In contrast, those who did not perceive clutter in their homes had lower levels of the stress hormone.

More time and energy

Living in a pleasant, decluttered environment will give you more zest and enthusiasm for life and help you be more active and social. Less time spent cleaning and tidying means more time for things that matter the most to you, be it family and relationships, hobbies, travel, health and wellness, or making plans for the future and pursuing your passions.

More space for children to play

If you have kids at home, they will be thrilled when the decluttering is finished and they have more space to play. Your newfound decluttering habit will also set a good example for them and encourage them to put their toys or games away when they're finished playing with them.

A more effective workspace

If you work from home, you'll become far more productive once you've edited your living environment. You'll be able to focus and concentrate and be calmer, more productive, and more creative. Even if you don't host meetings at home, your background in Zoom meetings can give a glimpse into your life — and if colleagues see clutter and junk behind you, they might judge.

---

[1] Darby Saxbe and Rena L. Repetti, 'For Better or Worse? Coregulation of Couples' Cortisol Levels and Mood States', *Journal of Personality and Social Psychology* 98, no. 1 (January 2010): 92–103, https://doi.org/10.1037/a0016959.

A place to entertain and welcome others

When you live in a cluttered home, the last thing you want to do is throw a party or invite friends over for dinner. But when you get your mess under control, you'll be able to entertain or arrange social get-togethers as often as you want without feeling self-conscious.

Financial savings

Decluttering and living a clutter-free life can save you money. You'll quickly find an appreciation for the things you have in your home — and you'll reduce spending as a result. You might also learn to live a more efficient life, which can save you money in the long run.

For example:
- Lost items — they'll no longer be lost!
- Duplicate items — you'll know what you have and won't need to purchase duplicates.
- Clothes — you'll rediscover a wardrobe you didn't know you had and realize that less is more.

Greater flexibility and mobility

When your home is filled with possessions, you might not even entertain the thought of relocating. The idea of moving so much stuff from one location to another can be intimidating. But decluttering can change your situation dramatically, leaving you free to be as mobile as you'd like. It can open up personal, professional, and financial opportunities for you.

CHAPTER 2:

A home that's your sanctuary

If your home drove you crazy before, you'll now love the time you get to spend there, feeling clean, tidy, and totally relaxed. It will be your retreat and your oasis, a place to come to at the end of a stressful day that leaves you feeling overwhelmed and fatigued. You might even take the occasional staycation in your home because the atmosphere is so peaceful!

Decluttering has a lot more to offer than meets the eye. Some of these benefits will resonate with you more than others, and you could certainly construct a compelling *why* statement from these perks alone, knowing that a glittering pot of gold lies at the other end of your decluttering rainbow. Think about what's most compelling to you, whether it's something discussed here or a reason of your own. It's up to you to figure out what's most meaningful to you and make it your driving force.

Transforming Your Initial Why into a More Meaningful Why

If someone asked you right now why you want to declutter your home, what would you say?

Here's a list of three common answers to this question:
1. "The sight of so much disorganization and messiness in my home bothers me, and I just can't live with it anymore."
2. "I'd like to live in a larger home with more space, but since I can't afford to move, I need to get rid of stuff to try to make our place feel bigger."
3. "I decided I didn't need everything I'd been holding onto and wanted to live life with fewer material things."

All these are legitimate reasons to declutter, and all can light a fire under you to take the first few baby steps. They're good starting points, but none go deep enough to be classified as an authentic *why*.

Even if you're working with the same reasons, your *why* statement might look completely different from the above examples because it will be linked to your core values and what drives you. It should be as unique as you are.

Let's take the three reasons for decluttering and convert them into *why* statements that relate this activity to your fundamental desires and motivations:

#1 Your reason for decluttering:
"The sight of so much disorganization and messiness in my home bothers me, and I just can't live with it anymore."

Your why statement:
"I want to declutter because the disorganization and messiness don't reflect the person I am and stress me out. I take pride in caring for myself and my family, and I want our home to show that. If I can get the clutter under control, I will feel like a weight is lifted off my shoulders."

#2 Your reason for decluttering:
"I'd like to live in a larger home with more space, but since I can't afford to move, I need to get rid of stuff to try to make our place feel bigger."

Your why statement:
"I want to get rid of the clutter in my home so I can have the space to live more happily with my family, think more clearly, and just relax instead of feeling boxed in and buried by the stuff surrounding me. Creating that space will open up possibilities in my life."

#3 Your reason for decluttering:
"I decided I didn't need everything I'd been holding onto and wanted to live life with fewer material things."

Your why statement:
"It's my experiences that matter the most, not the things I collect, and I want to get back to living a rich and exciting life filled with fantastic memories and amazing people."

Your *why* should motivate you. Once you figure it out, write it down and keep it front and center to remind you how important decluttering is to you and help you break free of the hold your possessions have on you.

KEY TAKEAWAYS FROM CHAPTER 2

- Your *why* is the core motivating reason connected to your purpose, something you do or want to do. Crafting your unique *why* will help drive you to fully declutter your home.
- There are many perks to decluttering, and they can help point you in the right direction if you're having trouble determining your *why*.
- Write down your personal *why* and read it often, especially when you feel your energy to declutter fading.

CHAPTER 3:

The Past and the Future

"Your past does not equal your future."
– TONY ROBBINS

How did you get here? Where do you want to go? We all have a past — and we can't change it. However, your future begins just one second from now, so how will you shape it? You can start now by creating a good decluttering plan. Preparation is the first step toward success.

You need to understand how much clutter you currently have and how it got there. When you have insights about your personal cluttering habits and tendencies, you can learn to recognize and control them in the future.

Don't worry if this sounds intimidating or scary — I'll walk you through it.

How Did All This Clutter Get Here?

Your clutter is stuff you brought into your home and purposely or inadvertently decided to keep or lost track of and held onto. Things you don't have space for and items that have lost meaning, relevance, or function feed the mess.

Files of papers and old mail have a way of sticking around. It's also not unusual for people to keep items like old refrigerators, TVs, or couches — they're bulky and not easy to dispose of. Then there's the problem of buying things — be it clothes, books, crafting supplies, or what have you — without editing what you already have. It's now time to explore your unique clutter tendencies so that you can address them.

Start by walking around your home. Go from room to room and open drawers, closets, cabinets, and storage bins — try to see the clutter you have become blind to over the years and think about what led to it.

There are a number of reasons you might have held onto things you once valued:

- Your plate has been full, and you just kept accumulating without finding the time or energy to declutter.
- You experienced a significant life event that temporarily left you without the time or energy to keep the clutter at bay.
- You're cautious and frugal by nature and reluctant to get rid of anything that you think you might use in the future.
- You downsized homes but didn't downsize your possessions.
- Your children are now older, but you've held onto baby clothes, preschool artwork, or other nostalgic items.
- You're naturally sentimental and tend to associate objects with treasured memories.
- You enjoy shopping and buy things faster than you dispose of them.
- You've collected memorabilia or souvenirs and have never gotten rid of them.
- You procrastinate and haven't had the time or desire to declutter.
- You're a perfectionist and can't find time to declutter as well as you'd like.

- You're indecisive about what to do with what you have, so you do nothing.
- You're afraid you'll regret throwing things out.
- It's actually your partner, live-in parent, or child that has created most of the clutter, and you haven't interfered out of love and respect.

No matter the reason, with focus and some behavior changes — like the tips and tricks discussed in later chapters — clutter is something that you can control moving forward.

As you make your "clutter assessment tour," take some notes for each room or area in your home. Decide how cluttered each room is compared to your expectations and make a quick note on why the clutter built up in that room. Take notes here or grab your notebook and track everything there.

Entryway:
MORE / LESS / SAME amount of clutter as I expected
Clutter built up here because: _____
_____

Kitchen:
MORE / LESS / SAME amount of clutter as I expected
Clutter built up here because: _____
_____

Living Room:
MORE / LESS / SAME amount of clutter as I expected
Clutter built up here because: _____
_____

Dining Room:
MORE / LESS / SAME amount of clutter as I expected
Clutter built up here because: _____
_____

Play Area:
MORE / LESS / SAME amount of clutter as I expected
Clutter built up here because: _____
_____

Bedroom 1:
MORE / LESS / SAME amount of clutter as I expected
Clutter built up here because: _____
_____

Bedroom 2:
MORE / LESS / SAME amount of clutter as I expected
Clutter built up here because: _____
_____

CHAPTER 3:

Bedroom 3:
MORE / LESS / SAME amount of clutter as I expected

Clutter built up here because: _____

_____

Office:
MORE / LESS / SAME amount of clutter as I expected

Clutter built up here because: _____

_____

Basement:
MORE / LESS / SAME amount of clutter as I expected

Clutter built up here because: _____

_____

Attic:
MORE / LESS / SAME amount of clutter as I expected

Clutter built up here because: _____

_____

Garage:
MORE / LESS / SAME amount of clutter as I expected

Clutter built up here because:: _____

_____

Shed:
MORE / LESS / SAME amount of clutter as I expected

Clutter built up here because: _____

_____

The exercise will help you see your clutter without rose-tinted glasses. Once you begin to see what needs to change, you can develop a plan to prevent the clutter from returning.

Where Is Your Home on the Clutter Scale?

Some homes are more cluttered than others. It's helpful to know where you stand on the clutter scale so you know how far you have to go to reach your decluttering goals.

To get a handle on reality, I like to classify clutter into four different stages, ranging from the mildest to the most severe.

Stage 0: Zero Clutter
Congratulations! No decluttering needed.

Stage 1: Enough to Notice
While a visitor might not notice the disarray, you notice it. There is clutter in more than one location, but everything still looks manageable. If you dedicated a weekend to decluttering, you could probably get it under control.

Stage 2: Enough to Cause Anxiety
You have clutter in enough different places that it has begun to stress you out and make you lose focus. However, it's still mild enough that you could hide a lot of the surface clutter in closets, cabinets, and under beds in a pinch if you needed to.

Stage 3: It's Everywhere
Clutter rests on just about every surface — and inside drawers, cabinets, or cupboards if you work up the nerve to open them. Disorganization has become your home's default state, but you can still move through the house without tripping.

CHAPTER 3:

Stage 4: Cluttered Up to Your Eyeballs
Clutter has overtaken your home, and some surfaces are completely covered. In some places, things are piled so high that it blocks windows and doorways. When you open the door to any room, it hits something that stops it from opening all the way. All in all, your home resembles the homes shown on hoarding TV shows.

Most of you are probably at Stage 2 or 3, with some parts of your home rating higher or lower. You can determine this for yourself as you go from room to room. Look at each room with fresh eyes, pretending you've never been inside and are seeing it for the first time. This will allow you to see the clutter that you may have previously learned to accept or ignore. You'll soon begin to develop an idea of how much work you'll have to do to get your home looking and feeling incredible.

The following chart can be used as you go from room to room. Rating the level of clutter and writing down thoughts about each room will help you later on when you create your decluttering plan. Try to make it a quick exercise — don't overthink it.

ROOM/ AREA	CURRENT	FUTURE GOAL	NOTES
	Clutter Stage (0 to 4)	Clutter Stage (0 to 4)	
Entryway			
Kitchen			
Living Room			
Dining Room			
Play Area			
Bedroom #1			
Bedroom #2			
Bedroom #3			
Bathroom #1			
Bathroom #2			
Office			
Garage/Shed			
Basement/Attic			

While some people want to completely eliminate their clutter, others are happy just to get their clutter level down to Stage 1. Someone starting out at Stage 4 might be satisfied to reach Stage 2. Decluttering is a process, and it might take a few rounds to get it down to the stage you're comfortable with.

CHAPTER 3:

Your decluttering preferences may vary by room or area, so you may want to reach Stage 0 (no clutter at all) in your living, dining, and bedroom areas, but be content with Stage 1 or 2 in your basement and garage. Even if you think you'd like to eventually get rid of all your clutter, it might be easier to do it in rounds until you're happy with how much is left.

Visualize It so You Can Achieve It

Before you can devise a plan, you need to know what you want to accomplish. One way to do this is through visualization. Visualization exercises are powerful tools you can use to help you identify long-term goals and reinforce the focus you need to transform your home and your life.

Step 1: Lie down in a quiet, comfortable place where you won't be disturbed for about ten minutes. Close your eyes and cover them with something soft to block the light.

Step 2: Take a few moments to relax and unwind, and then picture yourself taking a slow tour of your home. As you go from room to room, open every drawer, cabinet, cupboard, closet, and storage area and envision everything looking clean, orderly, and decluttered.

Step 3: Once you've completed your imaginary tour, picture yourself sitting in a comfortable chair, celebrating your freedom from the clutter that has been holding you and your family back and the physical and mental energy you now have.

After you've finished the visualization exercise, jot down a few notes to help you remember what you saw and how it made you feel. Then, go back to the clutter scale and evaluate where you would like to be once some of the clutter is gone. Make sure you set your expectations for your own home, and don't base your expectations on other peoples' homes or what you see on social media. Decluttering is about doing what works best for you and your family. Focus on what feels right, and be prepared to take the steps to make it a reality.

KEY TAKEAWAYS FROM CHAPTER 3

- Before diving into the task at hand, reflect on your cluttering habits. When you know why you've collected so many things, you'll have a better chance of changing your behavior to reduce clutter in the future.
- Rate the clutter in your home on the clutter scale, which objectively evaluates your decluttering needs.
- Everyone's tolerance for clutter is different, so think about how much stuff in your home works for you before you start decluttering.
- Don't base your expectations on others — set your own standards for an acceptable level of decluttering.

CHAPTER 4:

Setting the Stage for Success

*"We have two choices in life:
accept conditions as they exist or accept
responsibility for changing them."*

– ELAINE WELTEROTH

In our quest for a clutter-free life, we often overlook an essential element: planning. Yes, my friend, before diving headfirst into our mountain of things, we need a roadmap — and the roadmap you create in this chapter will get you to the decluttered home you're dreaming of. Without it, the journey will be chaotic and unproductive.

You're more likely to reach your goal if you have a written plan. It doesn't have to be overly detailed or complicated, but it should be a guide that takes you from start to finish and provides you with some form of accountability.

So, let's get that done so you can get started decluttering. The plan you make will be:
- Simple and uncomplicated
- A roadmap with goals and milestones to help keep you on track
- Time-bound with start and finish dates
- Flexible so you can adjust as you need to

3 Steps to Set Yourself Up for Success

When it comes to decluttering, you're creating order out of chaos. In my decluttering journey, I learned that three things are essential yet often overlooked:
1. You have to prioritize the decluttering.
2. It's essential to write a simple plan.
3. Use time blocking.

Prioritizing your decluttering project is critical — I can't stress this enough. Most of us are very busy, and finding time is difficult. It's easy to allow day after day to go by without starting, even though you know you need to take care of it.

Decluttering time is time you set aside, and you have to commit to it like you would commit to dinner with a good friend you haven't seen in years or an appointment with a doctor you've waited months to see. It might sometimes be necessary to deprioritize other things.

Another way you can prioritize decluttering is by eliminating or minimizing distractions when you plan to declutter. This might include:
- Turning off notifications on your phone. Whether it's a text, a call, or a social media notification, even a single ping on a phone can be enough to throw you completely off track.
- Setting boundaries by telling people you'll be busy and unavailable when you plan to declutter.

If you have children, this could also include:
- Getting a babysitter or asking your partner or a relative to take them out of the house when you're actively working on decluttering. You can also ask your partner to oversee carpooling the kids while you get to work.

CHAPTER 4:

- Working when your children are on a playdate, at school, or napping.

Write Down Your Plan

I'll guide you through exactly how to do this, and the good news is that if you did the exercises in the earlier chapters, you're already halfway finished!

Your plan will be your master roadmap that outlines the areas of your home you want to declutter. The rooms will be listed in the order you plan to work on them, along with start and end dates for each area. Keep it simple and on a single page.

Creating Your Plan

Four simple steps to create your plan!
1. Refer back to the notes from the exercises in Chapter 3, where you rated your clutter by room. Those notes will be your basic input to your plan.
2. Write your *why* at the top of the page, and then list the rooms or small areas of your home that you want to declutter in the order you'd like to work. Also, note the current and desired level of clutter by room.
3. Assign start and finish dates for each room (you can always change these dates later).
4. Build in celebrations and rewards for yourself when you hit milestones (even minor ones).

The decluttering order is up to you, but I have some suggestions. Start with an area that you can finish quickly — even if it means completing a corner of a room — so you can get a quick win under your belt. Starting in smaller spaces or

37

areas that aren't as cluttered builds positive momentum and gets those endorphins pumping. A drawer, small closet, or shelf are great places to start.

If you have a space that's really bothering you, and you're up for a larger task to start with — then use that motivation to tackle that area first.

If you start with a larger, more cluttered space, subdivide it into smaller bite-size pieces and work your way from one side of the area to the other. This way, you can make visible progress and move on to the next zone.

It can help to declutter closets and storage cabinets before decluttering the room connected to them. This will free up space so you can then put things away where they belong as you declutter the rest of the room. Sometimes clutter builds up because there's no space left in the closet.

Add in rewards for yourself for progress along the way, and write them into the plan. No one else is going to reward you, and it's important to give yourself credit and celebrate your accomplishments — even the small ones. And it doesn't have to be something costly or extensive. It could be watching your favorite show, indulging in your favorite snack, going for a hike, or spending an hour reading in your favorite coffee shop.

The following example can give you an idea of how your plan can come together.

Example:
Jessica's Home Decluttering Plan

My *why*: I want to declutter our house because we all work hard and deserve to live in a place we love, where we can unwind, have fun, and entertain.

Start Date: 6/3
Finish Date: 12/30

CHAPTER 4:

ROOM or AREA	Clutter Stage (Start)	Clutter Stage (Finish)	Start Date	End Date	Special Notes & Reminders	Reward or Celebration
Entryway	2	0	6/3	6/3		
Powder Room	1	0	6/3	6/3		
My Closet	3	2	6/4	6/5	Excited!	
My Bedroom	3	1	6/5	6/6	Drawers first to make space. Then do nightstands. Make it an oasis.	New sheets & duvet
My Bathroom	3	1	6/10	6/10	Dump out all old makeup and products. Get shelves for under the sink.	New bath towels
Living Room	3	1	6/28	6/29	Clear out the entertainment center to make space for holding what we need to keep.	Hire a handyman to hang artwork.
Kitchen	2	1	7/1	7/2	Focus: cooking utensils, plastic containers, & old bakeware	
Dining Room	2	0	7/3	7/3		Host July 4th party
Office / Craft Room	3	1	7/5	7/5	Get rid of old project materials.	
Linen & Utility Closets	3	2	7/31	7/31	Get rid of a lot so it's not overflowing.	
Upstairs Bathroom	2	0	8/1	8/1		
Lily's Bedroom	2	1	8/2	8/3	Work with Lily on this.	Back-to-school shopping
Molly's Bedroom	3	2	8/2	8/3	Work with Molly on this.	Back-to-school shopping
Garage	4	2	12/26	12/30	Whole family project	Plan a family adventure

Time Block

Let me introduce you to "time blocking," your new best friend on this journey. It's a simple concept that boosts productivity and keeps overwhelm at bay while decluttering. Time blocking is a time management and productivity technique that allocates defined segments of time to focus on specific priorities, tasks, or sets of tasks.

Breaking down the decluttering process into bite-size pieces makes it less intimidating and more achievable. With your master plan done, it's time to block out time on your calendar to put that plan into action. You can use a calendar, app, or phone reminder to reserve the time and remind you. Just be sure it's a system you'll see and won't lose track of.

On the first pass, time block only a few hours. As you get closer to the day when you're going to declutter your space, you can break down that single block of time into smaller blocks so you can work with focus and make real progress. I like to break the time into twenty-minute "sprint sessions" with some breaks in between. Sprint sessions are short periods of hyper-focused time. You can do one sprint session per day, or as many as you like. The sessions can be back to back or spread out at different times during the day.

If it's a day when I want to spend several hours working, I call it a "marathon session" — a series of sprint sessions strung together with breaks between each one. A "marathon session" is when you set aside a long period of time (perhaps half a day or a whole day) to declutter. If you're highly motivated and have a deadline you're working against, this can be a great way to make significant progress quickly. Mix up marathon session days with a few short sprint days, or take good breaks between marathon session days. Without breaks, you run the risk of burnout.

Here are some tips for how to schedule and use time blocks to your advantage:

1. Add your time to your calendar, write a schedule on paper, or use an app or other form of time planning and management.
2. Look at your plan and estimate how many hours you'll need (or want to take) each day.
3. Break larger blocks of time into twenty-minute segments. Be specific about what you will work on in each twenty-minute time block (for example, night tables, under the bed, or kitchen countertop).
4. Aim to finish a designated area in each time block. The goal is to use these finite periods of time to motivate you to finish each area you've committed to in each time block. You want to use time as a deadline to speed you along through the process.
5. If you don't finish your area in the dedicated time block, try again and find the balance between how long it realistically takes you to get through your stuff and how you can use the time block as a deadline to help you move more swiftly through your decluttering.
6. When working for more than one twenty-minute sprint session at a time, add short breaks in between — perhaps a three-to-five-minute break to get up, stretch, or take a bathroom break. When doing marathon sessions, you'll need a couple of longer breaks built into your day, like for lunch or a snack. Remember to stick to your schedule to stay on track, and don't make your breaks so long that you forget to get back to decluttering!

Time Blocking Jessica's Plan

Let's go through Jessica's plan from earlier to see how she could time block and get into action:

- She blocked off three hours of decluttering time on June 3rd to work on the entryway and powder room. Because

they're not very cluttered to begin with, that should be more than enough time.
- She blocked off four hours for day one of closet decluttering on June 4th, and then two hours on June 5th to finish up because sorting through the old clothes, shoes, and random things buried in there will take a bit of time.
- She'll continue marking all the key dates on her calendar and setting reminders on her phone.

When Jessica gets closer to the work days, she'll want to break her big block of time into smaller chunks to help her stay on task for the day. For example:

June 3rd Decluttering Plan
- 4 p.m. to 7 p.m.
- 4:00 – 4:20 – work
- 4:20 – 4:25 – break
- 4:25 – 4:45 – work
- 4:45 – 4:50 – break
- 4:50 – 5:10 – work
- 5:10 – 5:15 – break
- 5:15 – 5:30 – work
- 5:30 – 5:50 – eat a bowl of fruit and assess how much is done and how much more there is to do
- 5:50 – 6:10 – work and pick up the pace if need be
- 6:10 – 6:12 – break
- 6:12 – 6:32 – work and pick up the pace if need be
- 6:32 – 6:35 – break
- 6:35 – 7:00 – last burst of work before I'm done for the day

Jessica would then reassess what she had accomplished or didn't accomplish through her session. She would also note what she'll need to do for her next decluttering session. If she

CHAPTER 4:

underestimated how long it would take or didn't work quickly enough, she would apply what she learned from her experience to future plans.

You might not have to write down the twenty-minute time-block plan as shown here, but it gives you an idea of what it would look like. If it helps you to write it down, then go for it. Another way to keep you on track is to use a timer. Set a timer for twenty minutes, then set it again for your break period, and repeat. Do this not to box you in but rather to keep you on task and working efficiently and effectively.

Here are a few things to keep in mind as you get the hang of this:

- You'll likely get into a rhythm as you go, so you will become more efficient with time.
- If you find that you're consistently underestimating how much time you take with each task, then double the amount of time you think you'll need when you time block.
- Your plan shouldn't be stressful. It's meant to keep you on track with your milestones and goals.
- Use the time blocks to push you along and help you make decisions swiftly, but be careful not to push yourself too hard or to the point of burnout.

As you work on your plan and decluttering, don't procrastinate, but be realistic. The clutter didn't build up in a day, so you won't be able to completely get rid of everything in a day. However, with dedication and commitment, you can declutter much more quickly than it took to build up the mess.

Now you'll have to do the mental and physical work of decluttering, so don't let that live on your to-do list for long before you start working on it. Once you get going, you might be surprised how much it can affect your space and your life.

KEY TAKEAWAYS FROM CHAPTER 4

- Adjusting your mindset and making a plan will improve your chances of successfully overcoming your clutter.
- Relentlessly prioritize decluttering in your life, or else it won't get done.
- Write down a simple plan, including each room or area you want to declutter, and assign start and finish dates to each area.
- Use time blocking to break down your master plan into manageable segments of time that will keep you working effectively and efficiently without burning out.

CHAPTER 5:

It's Time to Declutter!

*"The first step in crafting the life you
want is to get rid of everything you don't."*

– JOSHUA BECKER

You can read all the books, make all the plans, and have all the conversations with friends about decluttering, but there comes a point where the planning must stop and action begin. It's time to start getting rid of that stuff you don't need to make space for what matters most.

A job with a plan is a recipe for success. When you create a written plan, you create a logical game plan for success. When it comes to decluttering, your game plan will be your schedule. It will outline general work time, short "sprint sessions," and breaks. The schedule will push you to success, motivate you to finish the task at hand, and remind you to pace yourself throughout the day.

Decluttering is a task that takes both time and energy. Many people begin their journey in high spirits, excited about their future home and its potential. However, they become overwhelmed, tired, and discouraged within minutes, hours, or days. Then they give up — ready to discard the whole idea in the bin intended for all the clutter they were not going to keep.

However, that is not what I want for you. You must stay motivated and energized while having the willpower and ability to push through even the most difficult situations and decisions. When it's time to quit for the day, I want you to feel pleased with yourself for all you accomplished — and excited to continue on. But how is this done? It's done by setting the stage right.

Time and again, I have found that the best time to start your decluttering process is at the very beginning of the day. It's those weekend mornings when you wake up with a full day ahead of you. As you jump out of bed, you feel the power of the day and are ready to charge forward.

Of course, this begins the night before by ensuring you go to bed on time to get the adequate amount of sleep you need to feel rested and ready to go. When you wake up, it's time to fuel yourself for the day — you need healthy foods, rich proteins, and your favorite morning beverage to perk you up. When you're well-fed, your mood and energy can be sustained, so as you go through your home decluttering throughout the day, you'll want to keep healthy, delicious snacks on hand. This could be your favorite seasonal berries, nuts, or protein sources like yogurt, nut butter, or hummus. Avoid sugary foods, which will spike your energy for a short while but bring you to a new low after it wears off.

Along with fueling yourself, keeping hydrated will help you stay energized and keep your mind focused. A 2 percent decrease in hydration can cause fatigue, memory loss, and mood swings. Stay fed and hydrated, and half the motivation battle will be won.

The next step is to create an enjoyable environment you can spend hours in. If music is your jam, crank up the tunes and have a dance party as you work. If audiobooks and podcasts are more your style, put on a new book or podcast episode and enjoy it as you work. To create a pleasant atmosphere, light a candle or add a diffuser (the smell will be relaxing and also mask some of the smells old things can produce) and set the room temperature so it's comfortable for working in for long periods.

Oh, and before you start, if you have allergies or are sensitive to dust, grab a mask to prevent the dust and allergens from interfering with your work.

Your motivation and energy are strong, so it's time to start decluttering! As you begin to sort through your things, it's important to be kind to yourself and take it one step at a time. The process itself is simple but not always easy. Difficult decisions will be made, and over and over again, you'll answer the question, to keep or not to keep? You'll have to be realistic with every item and decision you make. It may feel emotionally draining as you go through the sorting and decluttering process, but it's equally freeing. Every item you sort represents progress and is a step toward a tidier, more organized home.

The Ultimate Guide to a Tidy Home

This guide begins with the master plan (which you designed in previous chapters) of where you want to start your decluttering journey.

Step 1: The Room
The room you choose to begin with can be daunting because the entire process is new to you. You will need to learn to be ruthless with your belongings and learn the art of saying no. If a whole room is too difficult to tackle, focus on a single area, such as a pantry or hallway closet.

Step 2: Set Up a Work Area
Grab a folding table or find a flat surface that you can work on — and make it at least two feet off the floor so pets can't interfere with the process and your kids don't run into it or through it.

Tip: Find something around the home that will work, and don't buy anything new for the decluttering process — you want less stuff, not more!

Step 3: Create Sorting Stations
Grab eight bags or boxes (or a combination of the two) and a trash bin and label them as trash, recycle, donate, sell, shred, keep and return, and keep and move.

Next, you'll need Post-it notes or color-coding stickers in five different colors. These will be used to label larger items that don't fit the seven sorting stations. Assign a color to each of these categories: trash, donate, give away, sell, and keep.

Finally, grab a notebook and a marker for any notes you may need to make during the process.

Step 4: Start Sorting!
Now that you're set up, here is what you'll do with each station.
- *Trash.* Keep plenty of trash bags on hand; if anything is broken, chipped, old, used beyond repair, or expired, it goes in the trash.
- *Recycle:* Extra plastic and glass containers, cardboard, nonconfidential paper and mail, and similar products can be recycled in the appropriate bins or at your local recycling station. If in doubt, look for the recycle symbol — usually a green triangle and a number. If you're in doubt about whether something can be recycled, you probably should throw it out.
- *Donate:* If it's too good to throw out and you don't want to be bothered with selling it, that item goes in this box. Just be sure the boxes you use are sturdy enough to hold many things and won't fall apart during transportation. If the box is slightly weak, you can strengthen it by applying duct tape to the seams.

CHAPTER 5:

- *Sell:* If the thrill of a sale entices you, create a box (or area) to store the goods you wish to sell. The best way to sell products online is to make them a good deal — it will entice people to purchase. Drop the price in half or donate anything left after being for sale for over a week. You can always consider holding a yard sale if you have plenty of items.
- *Shred*: Anything slightly confidential from old mail to receipts goes in this box. Shipping services such as FedEx and many office supply stores offer shredding services. The price for these services can be free or based on weight.
- *Keep & Return:* If you still use the product and know you will use it in the future, put the item in this box. Once the area is sorted, swept, vacuumed, and wiped down, you can return the items to where they belong.
- *Keep & Move:* Place an item in this box if you intend to keep it but move it to a different room, closet, or area. Having a box for this category helps you get through decluttering without the interruption of leaving the room. At the end of the session, you can walk around to other areas of your home and return these previously misplaced items to where they belong.

Sorting Tips

At a basic level, everything needs to be sorted. If you sort through only half of your items, you'll still be stuck with clutter, preventing you from becoming decluttered and staying decluttered.

When you have all the items on your sorting table or area, organize them by category. This will help you spot doubles (or triples) of unused or unnecessary items. For example, if you are decluttering your kitchen begin by pulling out all the serving utensils. When you categorize the spoons, forks, pie servers, ladles, and so on, it becomes obvious if you have extras — and while six spoons may be helpful, it's doubtful that you need six pie servers. As a result, you can leave the spoons without a second thought but put at least four pie servers in the donation box.

At this point, take a step back, look at the items in front of you, and ask yourself, do I keep similar items elsewhere? Are there others you may have forgotten about in the bottom drawer of a chest or on the top shelf of a closet? If so, add them to the pile, as this will ensure you maintain a well-rounded picture of what you have.

Once everything is out in the open, start with the trash box and throw everything that's served its purpose here. From there, move to the donation pile. Hate it? Donate it. Don't use it? Donate it. Unnecessary duplicate? Donate it.

Once you've gone through the items to be trashed and donated, it's much easier to see what you have and start making decisions about keeping or selling things. Remember, feel free to continue adding to the trash and donate piles as you go.

As trash bags and boxes fill up, bring them to the dumpster. The feeling of physically throwing junk into the trash is extremely gratifying at this stage! It's instant feedback to yourself that your decision to tidy up your home is working. Similarly, if you plan on donating items, as the donation boxes fill up, move them to

CHAPTER 5:

your vehicle, community donation bin, or an area out of the way so you can clear them out of your home in the near future.

The last step in the process is to place the remaining items in the keep boxes. As you sort through what's left, don't be afraid to be ruthless in your decisions. Once your work area is empty, you've finished sorting! After you put the "keep" items back in their place, it's time to repeat the process in a different area of your home.

As you declutter, remember that you have limited space in your home for things to feel comfortable. The more you have, the more overwhelming your home can feel. At the end of the day, useless items in your home no longer serve you or your family. They may have been necessary or meaningful when you purchased them, but as we grow older and change, there comes a time when we must say goodbye to stuff. It's easy to throw out expired food, but when looking through your closet, hallway closet, or side table drawer, it can be difficult to distinguish between what has served its time and what may again be of use. For example, look at your closet. Some of us have a difficult time getting rid of items, even if they are worn-out or have become obsolete. Remember that even if a particular fashion comes back in style in ten or twenty years, it always comes back with a twist: a slightly different cut, material, or new color. While it's essential to keep a few staples and investment pieces — such as a black pencil skirt or blazer — you don't need to keep clothing just for "what ifs." Chances are your style and body composition will change long before the item comes back into fashion.

As you go through each area, do some light cleaning to help eliminate the dirt and dust before returning items to their places. However, at this stage, you'll focus on decluttering. Only when this has been accomplished will we start organizing. Decluttering will help you maintain a level of cleanliness in your home in the future — and it will make it more enjoyable as well!

Analysis Paralysis

During the first few rounds of decluttering, you may get stuck on whether to throw out an item. If you find this happening frequently, it's best to create another pile for "maybe" or "save for later." However, remember that when decluttering, the aim is to get rid of items and transform your home into a peaceful oasis that isn't weighed down by thousands of items.

As you go through items, make the process quick. Set a time limit for each area to force you to make quick decisions — this is where you can put your time-blocking schedules into effect. Limiting your time in each area will also motivate you to continue rapidly with the process. For example, set up your time blocks assuming that you will make only quick decisions and not loiter about as you weigh the pros and cons of each item. Never over-deliberate, and remember, if it's not a solid yes immediately when picking up the item, then it's probably best to say goodbye to it.

Finally, sometimes the decision has to be made by others — a spouse, child, sibling, or friend will often tell you their true thoughts about an item when you ask them whether or not to throw something out. When I first began decluttering several years ago, I struggled through my closet because I wanted to keep everything! However, my sister told me to toss 90 percent of the items I sent a photo of, and it really did help me to push past my analysis paralysis. Why? Because it taught me to look at things for what they really were rather than for their sentimental value.

Five Essential Questions

When you begin to declutter, it can be difficult at times to decide whether you should keep an item or it's time to let it go. These five questions will help you decide what to throw out or recycle,

CHAPTER 5:

what to donate, sell, or give away, and ultimately, what to keep. As Joshua Becker once said, "We were never meant to live life accumulating stuff. We were meant to live simply enjoying the experiences of life, the people of life, and the journey of life — not the things of life."

When you get stumped on what to do with an item, ask yourself these five questions.

1) When was the last time I used this?

To keep an item you don't love, it needs to be functional — that is, useful. I don't love a pan or a spatula, but they are helpful in my kitchen. I use them weekly, if not daily. Other items are used only seasonally — for example, Thanksgiving decor or birthday decorations. If you see yourself using seasonal items during the next season and have space for them, keep them. However, if an item hasn't been used in over a year, it is most likely time for it to go.

Related questions:
- If I use this product in the future, when will it be?
- Will this item serve its intended purpose when that time arises?
- How often did I use this item in the past?

2) Do I have duplicates?

Some items are useful to have duplicates of — dishes, clothing, books, and toys are all obvious acceptable duplicates. Collectible items you enjoy gathering as a hobby are also worthwhile keeping as long as you limit how many different types of things you collect because these can take up a lot of space and contribute to a lot of clutter. Duplicates accumulate quickly without us even realizing it, especially with kitchen appliances and personal care items. When dealing with duplicates, choose the item that serves you best and let go of the others.

Related questions:
- If I lost or donated this item, do I have something similar I could use?
- Do I have similar items that perform the same purpose?

3) Do I have space for this?

The main point of decluttering is to make room in your home for the things you actually use and to gain easy access to them. The point is not to reorganize your stuff so that it neatly stacks together and allows for more accumulation. You must come to terms with how much stuff you have and how much space you have. Decluttering is not "making" more space by rearranging shelves, purchasing organization containers, or finding creative ways to maximize your space. Instead, focus on the space you do have, get rid of what you really don't need or can't fit, and think about how much more effective organizing will be after you declutter and how much easier it will be to access everything when you get rid of 50 percent of the items.

Related questions:
- Do I really have space for this, or am I "creating" space to store it?
- Am I creating space or making excuses because I want to save this item?
- Does this item take up more space than it's worth?

4) Does this have emotional significance?

When an item has emotional, familial, or historical significance *and* you like it, then perhaps it deserves space in your life. However, if the object invokes negative emotions or a feeling of indifference, then there is no use in keeping it.

Items like wedding and birthday gifts can cause a sense of guilt rather than relief when throwing them out. However, if you never asked for the item, then rest assured no guilt needs to be involved. Never offer the item back to the person who gave you the gift, but rather just quietly put it in the donation or trash bin and move on with life. For items from parents or friends you wanted but no longer use, take a photo to remember it and then move it to the appropriate box.

One thing to be cautious about — never assume someone will want the item after you die. This may be an extreme thought, but it's realistic, so bear with me. Just because something is important to you doesn't make it important to them, and saving an item or family heirloom for the next generations is not a reason to keep it. If in doubt, you can ask family members to help you figure out whether you should keep or let go of an item or collection of items.

Related questions:
- Am I keeping this to make others happy?
- Does this item still play a role in my life, even if it's no longer used?

5) Does this align with my future goals or lifestyle vision?

You started on your decluttering journey because you realized that the way you currently live — surrounded by stuff — is no longer working for you. Keep that in mind as you evaluate your stuff and envision how it would fit into your home when you are done decluttering. If you're aiming for a minimalistic or modern style, will this item align with that goal? When you declutter, focus on the here and now and not the distant future, maybes, and perhaps.

Related questions:
- Does this item fit in with the space?
- Does this item fit in with my life now?

Keeping Items

When you decide to keep something, you acknowledge that the item brings value to your life and home — it has a role to play. Whether they're useful or bring a smile, the items you choose to keep are there because you want them. The only things you should keep that you don't necessarily want are current medications and critical paperwork or documents. Beyond that, I can't think of any other reason to keep an unwanted item.

Recycling and Responsibly Disposing of Items

Just because something is trash doesn't mean the only place for it is the trash can. We live in a very wasteful society, so I'm a big fan of reducing my carbon footprint when possible. If you can't reuse an item, it's best to give it to someone who can if you're able. If reusing doesn't work, then recycling is a good option. Some plastics, cardboard, and glass are easy enough to recycle in your weekly recycling bins — and please do.

Electronic waste (e-waste) can be more difficult to dispose of. However, most communities or municipalities will have e-waste events a few times a year. In the interim, office supply stores often take items like printers and fax machines to refurbish and resell.

Clothing can be recycled through recycling programs. Certain textiles, such as wool, can be recycled (ask at a local fabric store or post wool sweaters for free on Facebook Marketplace, as some people love unwinding the thread and reusing it!). Some retailers, such as H&M, and mail-in programs, such as Thread Up, also accept gently used clothing. In the US, textiles can be recycled through local textile refurbishment programs, which can be identified at nysar3.org/textile_recovery_locations.php, and in Canada at nactr.ca/donation-site-locator/. Kelsea

CHAPTER 5:

Schumacher, a researcher at the National Institute of Research and Technologies, says, "Textiles are one of the fastest growing categories in the waste stream." Let's not be part of that cycle!

Other types of programs that aim more for safe disposal than recycling include medication disposal services (especially for expired medicine and needles) at most pharmacies, safe disposal of batteries at many grocery stores, and city-run annual toxic cleanups (for oil, lubricants, paints, other toxic substances, and e-waste).

Donating Items

One of my favorite ways to dispose of unwanted items is to donate them. Many secondhand stores today cater to specific causes: Alzheimer's, breast cancer, animal shelters, women's centers, churches and missions, food banks, and more. When donating to particular charities, you'll allow others to purchase the item, and the profits go to causes near and dear to your heart. It's an excellent way to support charities when you don't have the resources. And you may get a tax benefit from your donation as an added bonus.

You can also donate specific items to specific locations. Some of my favorite places to donate to are:
- Homeless shelters: jackets, boots, hats, gloves, pants, shirts
- Food banks: unexpired food and drinks
- Pregnancy care or women's centers: jackets, maternity clothing, baby clothing, baby gear and supplies
- Children's hospitals: brand new toys
- Habitat for Humanity: furniture, appliances, and equipment
- Planet Aid: linens in good condition
- Animal shelters: older blankets, towels, pet supplies in good condition
- Libraries and schools: books in like-new condition

Donating items to places like those just listed makes the decision to let go of an item much easier. These things are getting a second chance at life and can change someone's life for the better. Just ask yourself, can someone benefit from this item more than me?

Giving Away Items

Giving items to friends and family is different from donating, although arguably the two do go hand in hand. When you give away items, be sure they are nice, current, and truly useful. You don't want to clutter someone's home with the stuff you couldn't bear to donate or throw away. Items you give away should still have lots of life left in them and continue to serve their purpose. For example, you could give away baby and kid's clothing, shoes, and toys to family, friends, and neighbors or post it on Facebook groups.

When you offer items for free and no one grabs ahold of them, it's a sign to get rid of them by donating, recycling, or trashing them. As a general rule of thumb, if no one claims it for three days, get rid of it.

Selling Items

As I've mentioned before, the point of decluttering is to get rid of unwanted stuff as soon as possible to make your life easier, more peaceful, and more productive. Going through the hassle of selling hundreds of items may not necessarily align with the decluttering mindset as it could slow you down. However, there may be times when it makes sense to sell, especially if you're looking for a few extra dollars to spend on organizational systems or if it helps to keep your motivation rolling.

CHAPTER 5:

Today, one of the most popular places to post items is on Facebook Marketplace. Bigger ticket items and furniture in great condition often move quickly. Another option is to host a garage sale. Setting a date for a garage sale motivates and boosts my decluttering progress quickly because I'm against a deadline. It's even more enjoyable and effective when I do it with a friend in the neighborhood. I have found it very gratifying to get so much stuff out of our home in one day while also witnessing how others can benefit from it. As a bonus, garage sales are also a fun activity for my daughters, and they get to see the circular economy come to life while learning how to hustle in the process!

Your ultimate aim should be to get rid of your items with the secondary goal of making money. Whether selling online or in person, here are a few tips to get rid of your stuff quickly:

- *Set a low price to sell or accept the best offer.* You want the items out of your house, so price them accordingly. If the standard price of an item secondhand is $100, sell it for $50 or at the most $75. People love a bargain, and even if they aren't looking for the item, they may buy it just because it's a good deal. The items will be gone in no time — and you can go back to decluttering.
- *Set time scales.* Items sold online should be discounted by 50 percent every week. At the end of the month, take them off the website and either send them to the trash or donate them. Remember, you want the stuff *gone!* When having a garage sale, cut the price of everything by 50 percent past noon and give things away for free after 2 p.m. Leave time at the end of the day to bring what's left to a donation center. Never bring what's left back into your home.
- *Clean it.* If it's dirty, take a minute or two to shine it up. No one wants to bring your dirt into their home. Plus, it sells better when it's clean.

The ultimate objective of selling quality items is to move them from your home quickly and efficiently. Some people love selling things — it comes naturally to them, and they get a thrill from the process. Others dread it, finding it complicated, intimidating, or unappealing — if this sounds like you, then don't bother with selling it. Donation and charity centers would be more than happy to do it for you!

Moving Forward

As you begin to declutter, many items will bring back memories and stories. However, don't let this distract you from the task at hand: decluttering. As another famous saying goes, a journey of a thousand miles begins with a single step. Although decluttering is much easier than walking a thousand miles, it does begin with a single step. And to finish the process, you must continue to put one foot in front of the other, sorting through one item at a time. Within hours, you'll notice a huge improvement in your home.

There are many, many options for what to do with all the excess stuff you no longer want or need. In this chapter, we discussed the various buckets that worked well in my home and that I established through trial and error; however, use whatever "buckets" or "boxes" you find most helpful and work for you. If you don't want to sell items, resort to a disposal system that works better for you, such as donating or recycling. If there are multiple places you could donate to, but it's too much work or you lack the motivation to keep decluttering after driving from place to place, then just find a general thrift store that would be happy to take it all off your hands. We've talked about various options and ideas — use the ones that work best for you, and maybe even motivate you, and declutter away.

CHAPTER 5:

KEY LESSONS FROM CHAPTER 5

- Begin the decluttering journey well-rested, fed, and hydrated, and aim to stay that way throughout the process. This will keep you motivated and energized.
- Set up a designated work area with a clean space for sorting, plus bags, boxes, and labels to control the area and make the process smoother.
- Use time blocking, leveraging bursts of energy to declutter, and then take breaks.
- Never be afraid to throw away items that no longer serve their purpose or your life.
- Just because an item doesn't serve your home doesn't mean it can't be of use to others. Consider donating, selling, and recycling unused items.

Decluttering Tip Sheet: TRASH or RECYCLE

Bathroom	• Old makeup, nail polish, perfume, toothbrushes • Old makeup brushes • Towels with holes • Expired medication • Hotel samples
Kitchen	• Expired food, herbs, spices, and cleaning supplies • Restaurant packets (salt, sauces, etc.) and menus • Chipped plates, cups, bowls • Broken appliances (e.g., waffle maker) • Cracked or chipped containers • Rusty pans and baking dishes • Extra plastic bags
Living room	• Old magazines • Pillows with rips and tears • Burnt-out candles
Office	• Old electronic cables that you're not sure what they belong to • Broken chairs and electronics • Used or partly used paper products
Playroom	• Puzzles and games with missing pieces • Broken toys • Fast food restaurant toys
Bedroom	• Socks that don't have a match • Anything with holes • Broken luggage • Novelty items you don't like (ugly Christmas sweaters, Halloween outfits) • Extra bed sheets that are never used

CHAPTER 5:

	Decluttering Tip Sheet: TRASH or RECYCLE
Paper supplies	• Restaurant menus • Manuals • Magazines • Receipts • Old mail, newspapers • Paid bills • Birthday cards • Business cards • Old notebooks, calendars, out-of-date materials • Craft supplies
Basement & Attic	• VCR and DVD players • Old furniture and supplies
Garage	• Old paint and stain, used paintbrushes • Oils, lubricants, fertilizers no longer used • Loose nails • Cracked and chipped flower pots

GET RID OF THE MESS

	Decluttering Tip Sheet: DONATE
Bathroom	• Curling irons and straighteners not used for more than a year • Old toiletry bags • Unused hair dryer attachments • Unused grooming products (nail trimmers, etc.) • Extra/unwanted body lotions, shampoos, soaps
Kitchen	• Duplicate utensils • Old recipe books • Excess baking dishes • Countertop appliances you don't need
Living room	• Extra blankets and pillows • Candles that are never burned • Extra artwork no longer enjoyed • Outdated home decor
Office	• Unused diaries, journals, and planners
Playroom	• Bulky toys • Toys and furniture no longer used • Board games and puzzles no longer used
Bedroom	• Old purses, shoes, clothes, hats, gloves • Clothes that haven't been worn in a year • Clothes that don't fit or you don't like
Basement & Attic	• Holiday decorations no longer used • Baby clothes and supplies (if no longer needed) • Unwanted "treasures"
Garage	• Duplicate tools • Unused sporting equipment

CHAPTER 5:

Decluttering Tip Sheet: KEEP *(items that are still used)*	
Bathroom	• Toiletries you still use • Good towels and linens
Kitchen	• All dishes, cutlery, pans, etc. that are in good condition and still used regularly
Living room	• Some sentimental items • Plants • Home decor
Office	• Essential documents
Playroom	• Toys still played with • Books
Bedroom	• Clothing that fits, is in good condition, and makes you feel good
Basement & Attic	• Family heirlooms and photos
Garage	• Tools still used • Sports equipment that's still used

CHAPTER 6:

Finding Motivation

"In order to do all those things that we know are good for us, we need to stop waiting and start doing."

— MEL ROBBINS

After a long day working at the office, then taking care of the kids, and finally settling in for a quiet evening, it can be difficult to find the motivation to begin decluttering or continue on from the night before.

When you set a goal, it's important to stay on top of it. Goal setting is worthwhile because it lays the foundation for the task and specifies the time you have. It's the fire that spurs you forward and sets you up for success. A big, overarching goal can be achieved by setting smaller goals and time scales like the time blocking we discussed in earlier chapters. Keeping the vision of your *why* will help you to stay focused on decluttering.

Accomplishing a task or goal boosts confidence, increases self-esteem, and brings more motivation for the next project. When goals are realistic, they help us stay on track and remain focused. When they're not, they are overwhelming and frustrating, and along with that comes dejection, a sense of failure, and erasure of any sense of motivation to continue pushing forward.

Mood boards always inspire motivation in me. When I was a teenager, I would cut and paste magazine images that I loved and desired to have one day — and today, I replicate that with Pinterest. Over time, my desires have changed, but I still love curating visuals to document my aspirations that help propel me into action.

If you need further motivation, create a vision of your home by developing a vision board or adding a photo file on your phone with inspirational photos of how you would like your home to look. Then, add photos of your own home and the areas you want to declutter. This will help you to see where you are now and where you want to go. After a day of decluttering, when your motivation begins to wane, look at the photos to see just how far you've come and capture the result of your work with a photo (and feel free to humblebrag with those before and after photos too!).

When my girls were younger, a picture of a neat and tidy playroom would inspire me to declutter their play area in our living room — a space that changed frequently over the ten years in which they went from toddlers to preteens, and with the number of gifts they got from family for birthdays and holidays, it was a room abounding with books and activities no matter how often I decluttered it. However, having a pretty living room was not my only motivation to declutter and organize their play area. My girls played better, were less overwhelmed by choice, and seemed happier when they weren't tripping over a toy dog or medical kit they were no longer interested in. Decluttering brought a sense of calm and order to the room.

What is your motivation? What makes you jump into action? Now is the time to revisit your *why* and reflect or build on it. Here's a reminder of some benefits of decluttering that may stimulate your motivation if you need more.

CHAPTER 6:

- *Less stress.* When someone is stressed, it creates a negative environment for everyone around them. It literally kills the joy in the home. When one person is stressed, everyone is stressed. After a long day of working, carpooling, and dealing with general life chaos, sitting down for the evening in a tidy, decluttered home brings a sense of calm and peace. My home is in order. I can rest here. The positive attitude brought on by my tidy home extends to my kids and husband, and it boosts our spirits.
- *Productivity.* When your home is void of excess stuff, it's much easier to focus and work and be productive. It also gives you the peace of mind to have work events at home or invite colleagues for meetings, events, or social events that will further those relationships.
- *Socializing.* Tuesday game nights. Friday night get-togethers. Family birthday parties. Holiday meals. We all have events throughout the weeks and months that we want to celebrate with friends and family. Entertaining others should never be accompanied by embarrassment that guests will notice piles of stuff in the living room corner or hang coats on chairs because the hall closet is overflowing. Decluttering will allow you to invite people over for an evening of fun without any awkwardness.
- *Children playing.* Despite what kids think and what toy companies tell us, kids play better with fewer choices. When kids have too many toys, they become overwhelmed, jumping from toy to toy before leaving it all behind because they can't focus. Excess toys take away from their creativity and serve only to entertain them rather than teach them how to play on their own. How many times have you bought a new toy only to find your child enjoys playing with the box it came in more?
- *Health.* Everything accumulates dust and dirt, even items stored at the back of the closet. In time, this creates a

- health risk for you and your family, not to mention that it, too, needs to be cleaned on a regular basis.
- *Home decor:* It's difficult to get excited about decorating a cluttered home. Once your place is free of clutter, you will finally be able to take your home to the next level, which can increase your gratification and happiness.

Your home should be the center of your world. At the end of the day, when you're cooking in the kitchen, you should feel the togetherness of your family or friends or the joy you get from cooking, if that's your thing. Your bedroom should be a peaceful place to lay your head. Your bathroom should have the sense of calm and cleanliness you want when you step out of the shower. Every room should be a safe, welcoming place that enables you to thrive — and decluttering will help you achieve that.

Your home is not about keeping up with the Joneses. Or your best friend. Or your colleagues. It should not be a place where you need to spend every waking hour cleaning excess things that are no longer needed. Don't try to meet other people's expectations — create your own. Chances are that most people don't think about you and your stuff. Declutter to make your own life easier and better.

Motivation Tips & Tricks

One thing that inspires many people's desire to declutter is watching decluttering and organizing shows such as *The Home Edit*, *The Gentle Art of Swedish Death Cleaning*, and Marie Kondo's Netflix series. Extreme shows like *Hoarders* are enough to scare most people into decluttering immediately! No one wants their home to get to such a state, but to prevent that, you must start modifying your behaviors and taking action to begin your decluttering journey. Decluttering can be difficult, but no one ever regrets doing it. Take the time to change your habits today so that tomorrow is a better day. Do it for your future.

See the Possibilities

A few years ago, my daughter and I walked through some open houses in the neighborhood. The houses were similar in size to ours, and as we strolled through one particular home, my daughter and I fell in love with it. My daughter told me that we just had to buy this home, with all the drama that only a ten-year-old can add! While I, too, was enamored with the house, I was able to see that it simply would not work for our needs. Yes, there were some things in it that I loved more than the house I was in — the extra bathroom, slightly larger kitchen, and more open spaces were all very appealing. However, the living area was smaller, and so were the bedrooms. As I pondered over the house, I realized that with some serious decluttering, a bit of reorganization, and better coherence in decor, I could make my home every bit as appealing as the open house was. And as a bonus, it could be done for a lot less money! You see, open houses are a great way to show you how beautiful a home can be with less stuff. It can paint a picture of what your future could look like without having to move.

Social media and online communities have become a vast source of inspiration for many of us — Pinterest, Houzz, Instagram, and real estate sites can inspire you to transform your home into a tidy, organized sanctuary. But a bigger house or fancier furniture will not bring you joy if you bring all your excess baggage with you. Possessions don't make us happier. Yes, they can make our lives easier, and they can bring a moment of satisfaction, but overall, can they truly make us content with our lives?

As much as the internet can be an inspiration, don't let it be your downfall. We can spend hours dreaming about better things and going down rabbit holes. We can spend months researching but never actually start on the task at hand. Do the research, but set a time limit (like thirty to sixty minutes), and then get started. If you need this type of inspiration, use it as a reward. For example, spend ten minutes on Pinterest (set a timer), and then get started. Half the battle is starting, so just start!

My tactic of creating a mood board (also known as a vision board) works for some people. A visual reminder of your desires can motivate you to begin or continue. Place it in a prominent place that you often walk by, such as the refrigerator door or bathroom mirror, and it will continue to motivate you throughout your day.

When you start decluttering, the idea is not perfection but just less stuff. It can be much easier to get your head around this and make progress, and it will fuel motivation. Setting your eye on unattainable perfection is more likely to set you up for struggle, disappointment, and burnout. While this can be an internal struggle for me, I talk myself through it and go for action over perfection any day.

Let other people know about what you're doing and how excited you are to change your home for the better. It can be your spouse, family, friends, or colleagues — let them know, and let them keep you accountable to your plan. It might even make you more excited! But even better, they can encourage you and maybe even give you tips and tricks for what worked for them in the past.

The satisfaction of taking action and accomplishing goals is a great feeling. It's the sign of a day well spent, and it gives you further motivation in your journey. It may even encourage your spouse and kids to do the same. Let them join in on the fun and declutter their personal spaces as well. We'll discuss that more in chapter eight.

CHAPTER 6:

Don't lose sight of your goals and dreams, and continue to reward yourself as you make progress and hit your milestones. Let accomplishment and victory be your inspiration and drive to declutter your home. Start today, even if you start small. Focus on the task at hand, and you will make progress.

KEY LESSONS FROM CHAPTER 6

- Get started on your decluttering journey — don't wait, as that will only postpone a better future.
- Tap into your *why* and seek out additional sources of inspiration if you need them, especially visual inspiration through social media or online.
- Watching home organizing shows can help motivate and inspire you.
- Use visual inspiration like mood boards if that helps you.
- Reward yourself as you make progress to keep your motivation up.

CHAPTER 7:

Working through Roadblocks and Maintaining Momentum

*"You may encounter many defeats, but
you must not be defeated."*

– Maya Angelou

You've started decluttering... and now you're back on the couch, frustrated with the clutter surrounding you and lacking the motivation to continue. Negative thoughts creep in, making you doubt yourself and your intentions. How do you move on from here?

We all face fears and doubts when we begin decluttering. As obstacles and pitfalls arise, procrastination, decision fatigue, and feelings of overwhelm can arise. Anyone who has decluttered for any amount of time has faced these feelings, myself included. However, with every roadblock, there are ways to push past them. And I will share the processes and strategies to do just that with you. But before we get to that, we need to discuss the roadblocks you might encounter while decluttering.

For some people, the biggest roadblock is overcoming the thought of letting go of potential treasures and the comfort they provide — "I might need this in the future" or "I bought that with my husband on our first trip together." For others, insecurity, sentiments, and indecision may prevent them from decluttering.

Sometimes time can be an obstacle. The time to plan, schedule, and declutter each and every area can be nonexistent in the midst of a busy schedule. Or it might take much longer to do than you initially thought.

Most homes have at least four rooms: kitchen, living area, bathroom, and bedroom. Add in all the other possible rooms — extra bedrooms and bathrooms, office, garage, basement, attic — and where does one start? The entire home needs to be decluttered, but choosing just one room (or area of a room) can be overwhelming. In earlier chapters, we discussed the decluttering process and the need to create schedules. If you lack time, jump back to chapter four for tips on making the time you need for the process. If systems and processes are confusing you, revisit chapter five. Rereading these chapters to help you overcome those obstacles is perfectly fine.

Even with a plan, you can still encounter challenges and roadblocks. You will be faced with many decisions, and at times, it won't be easy to decide whether or not to keep something. Have any of the following questions held you back?

- Do I really need to declutter?
- Can't I just live my life the way it is?
- Is this item important to me?

Before we dive into how to overcome particular roadblocks, ask yourself why you are running into them. Do you have negative feelings about the whole process? If so, try to look forward to a future with a tidy home. Do you dread the work involved? Then, break the work into small blocks and look at the process as a learning and growing opportunity. Have you tried decluttering before and failed or just given up? Today is a new day, offering a new opportunity to improve your home.

CHAPTER 7:

Question & Answer Exercise:

1. What is holding me back from wanting to declutter my home?

_____
_____
_____
_____
_____

2. What potential roadblocks will I face?

_____
_____
_____
_____
_____

3. How can I motivate/reward myself to overcome the roadblocks?

_____
_____
_____
_____
_____

When you take a moment to think through potential downfalls in advance, you can mentally prepare yourself for them, decreasing your chances of giving up. Just like having a plan to complete the job, it's also wise to plan for potential issues you may face. Then, when you do overcome the challenges, it will be much more motivating to continue to create a home in which you and your family can thrive.

Common Roadblocks

Over the years, I have noticed several common roadblock themes while aspiring to declutter.

Overwhelm

When people are overwhelmed, it can be difficult to think logically and in a way that can mitigate or overcome the situation. Feelings of overwhelm can arise when you think you have too much stuff to go through or don't know where to start. This can be linked to having a lot of things or sometimes to past negative experiences with decluttering, tidying, or cleaning.

Keep in mind that every person is unique, and so is their brain. Your brain processes objects and emotions differently than does your partner, friend, or neighbor. Therefore, while it may be easy for some to declutter, it can seem impossible for others. I have found that just getting rid of a few "easy" things can help kick-start the process and give you the confidence to begin.

CHAPTER 7:

Exercise: Decluttering Challenge

Step One: Grab a box to add items for donating.

Step Two: Set a timer for five minutes.

Step Three: Add one item you're willing to part with from each of the following categories:
- One mug or coffee thermos
- One book or magazine
- One accessory (purse, shoes, necklace)
- One clothing item
- One toy or game
- One decor item
- One item from the bathroom

Step Four: Ask yourself which item was the easiest to add. The location the easiest item came from might be the area you start with.

At this point, you may realize you need to adjust your schedule and begin with an easier area. This is totally fine! Build your confidence, and go through the sorting process once. After that, jump back to the schedule and work your way through it.

As you navigate through the challenge, remember to keep to very small areas and short sprint sessions with a twenty-minute maximum at a time. You can also limit the sessions to one per day for four to five days to build your "decluttering muscle"!

Perfectionism

Whether it's an inherited tendency or you've spent far too much time online looking at picture-perfect homes without a speck of clutter, you, as a perfectionist, can find that the amount of stuff surrounding you while decluttering is paralyzing. As can be the desire to have everything perfect on the first try.

When you feel your perfectionism beginning to overtake you, try one of the following tips to help you overcome it.

- Stick to your schedule and follow the time-block planner you created for the job.
- Create a list of what you want to do. Fight the urge to "go the extra mile" and perfect it.
- Force yourself to start when you find yourself thinking and planning too much.
- Reevaluate your goals and make sure they're realistic. If you're unsure about your list, ask a friend or your spouse if they think it's reasonable.
- When you fail to complete a list or don't think you've done your best, look at it from a growth mindset rather than as a failure.
- Focus on enjoying the process and embrace the outcome, regardless of what it may be.
- Practice identifying the thoughts you have that enable your perfectionism and come up with alternate thoughts (you'll find some examples of this as you read on).

CHAPTER 7:

Exercise: Reflection Journaling

Write a self-reflection about how decluttering will improve your life if you begin today rather than waiting for the perfect time or plan.

_____
_____
_____
_____
_____
_____
_____

Next, write about why you are going to focus on *completing* the job rather than on perfection.

_____
_____
_____
_____
_____
_____
_____

What Ifs

Your thoughts can be overpowering, and sometimes distractions that send you down rabbit holes can cause you to question every decision. "What if" questions are often linked to clothes, kitchen items, or tools, but they are also frequently connected to paperwork and records such as documents, old address books, and unused work files.

As a general rule of thumb, keep all taxes and government-related content for at least seven years, but check with your local government agency to confirm this. All paperwork related to homeownership should be kept permanently.

Exercise: Question and Answer

1. If I'm unsure of what to keep regarding paperwork, who can I ask?

_____

_____

_____

_____

2. Can I transfer potentially useful documents to a digital system?

_____

_____

_____

_____

3. How likely is it that I will need this paperwork again?

_____

_____

_____

_____

4. If I needed to buy a replacement item, how much would it cost? Is there anyone I can borrow this from (e.g., neighbors, friends, local community groups, etc.)?

_____

_____

_____

_____

Scarcity Mindset

We have all done it a time or two: spent way too much money on an item we seldom use (or never used to begin with). As a result, the thought of throwing out or donating an item that we spent money on but never benefited from can be frustrating. It's like throwing money in the trash can.

Scarcity mindset also comes into play with your relationship with money, and it can be deep-seated. You might fear not having enough if you let go of your physical possessions. You may worry about not having enough clothes or enough money to add to your wardrobe in the future. While I don't want you to get rid of your essentials if your financial concerns are real, oftentimes this is a matter of reframing the reality of the situation and how you think about your concerns.

Exercise: Self-examination Questions

1. Can I sell the item to recoup some of the costs?

_____

_____

_____

_____

2. Would I repurchase the item if I had the opportunity today?

_____

_____

_____

_____

3. How likely will I need a replacement for this item in the future? And if I don't have the money for it, how bad is the consequence? Is there an alternative to purchasing a replacement?

_____

_____

_____

_____

CHAPTER 7:

Sentimental Feelings

Memories and emotional attachment can make it difficult to part with a particular item. When items are given to you by a loved one, remind you of a loved one, or are made just for you, it can be challenging to part with them. These items can be related to both good and bad experiences and situations.

Exercise: Sorting through Sentimental Items

Ask yourself the following questions, and if you answer "yes" to any of them, you can probably skip the decision fatigue and get rid of the item.

- Did this person give similar items? Can I keep an item or two and let go of the rest?
- Does this memory have photographs to remember it by?
- Could I take a photo of the item and remember it that way?
- If this is part of a collection of sentimental items surrounding a person or time in my life, can I do something with a subset of the items in a way that would commemorate and honor the memory instead of keeping everything?
- Is this item holding me back?
- When I was given the item, was I obligated to use it?
- If this item is a family heirloom, is there someone who would value it more than I do?

Indecision

Indecision often arises when there are too many things to sort through or when you don't know where to store or display an item. Whether or not to keep something can be related to a host of concerns, from sentimental to financial, and these may influence your desire to keep the item. As a result, it may seem easier to defer the decluttering process, stall by decluttering another area, or procrastinate by switching to a different chore. Worst case scenario, it can lead to giving up altogether.

Exercise: Asking Others for Help

Find someone you trust — your spouse, child, or friend — and ask them for honest feedback about a particular item you are unsure whether to keep or throw out. Follow their choice, then set a timer (max thirty seconds) and try to make the next decision yourself. Repeat the process with each item until you can make every decision. As part of this exercise, you'll have to take direction from others and push yourself to be open to letting go.

When figuring out where to keep an item — if, in fact, it is a keeper — some of that will naturally become easier as you declutter your home and uncover new space. If you still need help figuring out where to put something, the following section will walk you through roadblocks.

Walking through Roadblocks

Once you learn to recognize when you've hit a roadblock, it becomes much easier to work through it. Roadblocks begin in your thoughts and often circulate around doubts and fears about keeping or getting rid of an item. When you hit a roadblock, read through the previous section or the following chart about how to reframe your thoughts so that you can continue to make progress.

Reframing your thoughts is a process whereby you take a negative thought and think about it in a new and realistic way. For example, in the following chart, the reframed thought is your "alternate thought," and it should always be related to the situation, challenge your current thought, and be realistic, believable, and readily understood. The decision should be a logical flow of the thought process.

In the process outlined here, the alternate thoughts and actions have the potential to turn inactivity and standstill to progress. When you declutter, your aim should be progress and not perfection. When you hit a unique roadblock, identify the thought associated with that roadblock and devise an alternative thought around it. Repeat that thought to yourself, and then proceed to act on it.

As roadblocks come up, be sure to write them down — that might be enough to come up with a quick solution to the problem. After that, brainstorm alternative thoughts and write those down too. Keep your notebook close by when you declutter so that you can rethink roadblocks as quickly as they arise. If you find it happening often, repeat the alternative thoughts to create mantras to overcome potential issues. You'll get better with practice!

GET RID OF THE MESS

	OVERCOMING CHALLENGING THOUGHTS AND ATTITUDES	
	Thoughts that hold you back	**Alternate thoughts to tell yourself** (a.k.a. think this instead)
Overwhelm	"I'm overwhelmed."	"I'm feeling totally overwhelmed, but I can do this if I just take it one small step at a time."
	"I don't know how I'm going to get through this."	"I'm capable of making a difference in the clutter I just need to work on it little by little."
	"I don't even know where to start."	"I'm feeling overwhelmed, but if I follow the steps in this book or ask for help if I need it, I'll be able to make progress with my clutter."
	"This is too hard."	"It feels really overwhelming, but I don't have to clear all the clutter at once. I can handle one little piece at a time."

CHAPTER 7:

OVERCOMING CHALLENGING THOUGHTS AND ATTITUDES

	Thoughts that hold you back	Alternate thoughts to tell yourself (a.k.a. think this instead)
What if?	"What if I need it later?"	"I probably won't need this later, but if I do, I can always get another one or borrow one from a friend."
		"Chances are low that I'll need this in the future, and while I want to hang onto it just in case I do, it's not worth it because it will just add to the clutter that I dislike so much."
		"I might need this again in the future, but chances are low, and if I keep it, then I might not even be able to find it when I do because it will be buried in clutter from not letting things like this go."
		"I might need this again in the future, and if I do, it might be a little bit of a problem if I don't have it anymore, but not getting rid of all of these things that I *might* need one day will end up being more of a problem."
	"What would my son/daughter like in the future?"	"I should not expect my children to appreciate items I've saved if they aren't attached to them or the meaning surrounding them."

OVERCOMING CHALLENGING THOUGHTS AND ATTITUDES

	Thoughts that hold you back	Alternate thoughts to tell yourself (a.k.a. think this instead)
Scarcity mindset	"I spent so much money on it, so I can't get rid of it (or I feel guilty getting rid of it)."	"Although I spent money on this, and it feels wasteful to get rid of it, I don't need it. Keeping it only contributes to my clutter, which causes other problems for me."
		"While I might feel like I'm throwing money out by getting rid of these things I spent good money on, I don't really use/need them, and keeping them costs me in other ways (time, health, and peace of mind)."
		"I need to get rid of things because I have too much stuff. I can actually save money by being choosier about what I purchase. That way, I will have enough to buy the things I really need in the future."
		"I feel guilty for buying this and never using it, like I'm wasting my money. However, I'm not using it, and holding onto it just reminds me of something that makes me feel bad. Getting rid of it will help me move on, and I can be more mindful of my purchases in the future."
	"If I get rid of this, I won't have the money to replace it if I need it."	"I don't have to spend money on lots of things in the future — just on what I really need. With these new spending habits, I should be able to afford what I need in the future."

CHAPTER 7:

OVERCOMING CHALLENGING THOUGHTS AND ATTITUDES

	Thoughts that hold you back	Alternate thoughts to tell yourself (a.k.a. think this instead)
Sentimental feelings	"I can't get rid of this because it was a gift."	"I can still be sentimental and care about the memory even if I don't keep the object/stuff attached to the memory."
	"I can't get rid of this because it brings back memories of a difficult time in my life."	"I'm holding onto this because it reminds me of a negative thing that happened to me in the past. I don't ever want to forget it, but keeping this isn't helping me heal and move forward. By getting rid of this, I actually can start to let go of the pain."
	"I can't get rid of this because it reminds me of a time when I was really happy."	"I'm so grateful to have these happy memories, but I don't need all of these things because they're taking up the space I need to live my life today and feel my best. Even if I let go of the things attached to the memory, I will always have the happy memories, plus the space I really need right now."
	"I will offend the person who gave this to me if I get rid of it."	"Even though I feel like the person who gave this to me would be offended if I got rid of it, they probably won't know I did so. And even if they did, they probably would expect that I would have gotten rid of it by now." "If I had given this to my friend, they would have definitely thrown it out by now, so they wouldn't be offended if I got rid of it."

OVERCOMING CHALLENGING THOUGHTS AND ATTITUDES

	Thoughts that hold you back	Alternate thoughts to tell yourself (a.k.a. think this instead)
Indecision	"It's too hard to decide what I should keep or get rid of."	"I can efficiently make decisions to get rid of things when I declutter because I know the good it will do for me far outweighs any potential mistake I might make by accidentally throwing something out that I might need or want in the future."

CHAPTER 7:

OVERCOMING CHALLENGING THOUGHTS AND ATTITUDES

	Thoughts that hold you back	Alternate thoughts to tell yourself (a.k.a. think this instead)
Perfectionism	"I can't get it to look perfect."	"I'm excited to start clearing out my clutter. If I just start and work through the process, my home will be in much better shape than if I overthink it and try to come up with the perfect plan of what to get rid of and how to organize."
	"It has to look perfect."	"Even though I get caught up thinking that my home should look "perfect," letting go of that expectation will actually help me make more progress in decluttering and cleaning up."
		"I feel like my home should look perfect, but the reality is it looks far from perfect now. If I keep putting off decluttering until I have the perfect plan, supplies, or moment, it will continue to get worse instead of better. Imperfect progress will help me so much more than waiting for perfection."
	"It's not worth going through this if I can't get it to look perfect."	"The decluttering process does not have to go perfectly to get my home to a place where it looks and feels much better than it does now."
	"I might make mistakes or throw something away that's important when I get rid of the clutter."	"Mistakes could happen, but a tidy home will be worth it. If I throw something out by mistake, the benefit of getting rid of the mess will likely outweigh the cost of a mistake."

	OVERCOMING CHALLENGING THOUGHTS AND ATTITUDES	
	Thoughts that hold you back	**Alternate thoughts to tell yourself (a.k.a. think this instead)**
Environmental guilt	"I feel guilty getting rid of this because I'm just adding to the landfill."	"While I feel bad that I'm adding to the landfill as I get rid of stuff, I can take steps to be as responsible as possible in the process and also change my ways moving forward to lessen my environmental footprint." "Throwing out so much stuff makes me feel guilty because I think about the impact on the environment. However, while it's important to think about my impact on the environment, I also need to think about taking care of myself, and cleaning out what I have is part of that. Instead of throwing everything out, I can donate or responsibly dispose of what I have to minimize environmental impact, and I can be more mindful of what I choose to purchase in the future."

CHAPTER 7:

Other Underlying Challenges

Decluttering is challenging, and sometimes you can lose interest before you get through it all. When this happens, remind yourself that you decided to embark on this journey. Take a moment to revisit your *why*, and look again at your mood board and all the "before" photos to see how far you have come.

Challenges are inevitable, but keep pushing forward, one item at a time. After long periods, even if you have found the process relatively easy, you may lose interest or become tired of all the decluttering. Many find this to be true with chores. After all, we have hectic lives, and when adding a task the size of decluttering room after room, there comes a time when you need a break. When you get tired, your body naturally wants to preserve energy and rest to rejuvenate. When we decide to climb a mountain in a day, it's an uphill battle — quite literally! Decluttering is both physically and mentally challenging, and if you've never done it before, then you have a lot of hills to climb without being "physically fit" for it. Give yourself grace and take breaks as you work. Stick to the schedule you planned and adjust as needed — this will keep you from setting unrealistic expectations for yourself.

When you begin to lose interest or get tired, ask yourself why. Was the task too much, or did you not pace yourself? Sometimes you need a fifteen-minute break to relax and recharge. Just make sure to get up and keep going after the break! I have found that when you begin to lose interest in the process, it's important to think of the reward at the end: a tidy home. Look back at your *why*, and pin a few photos to the wall of your inspiration to keep the motivation going. If you have particular doubts or worries, refer to the chart we discussed earlier to reframe your thoughts and keep going.

If you struggle to stay focused, rely on your schedule and create smaller lists of things you need to do or come back to. Every time you accomplish a point on your list, mark it off and let it be a visual reminder and your motivation to continue. You can also attach other rewards to your progress to help you keep going. Another option is to schedule twenty-minute sprint sessions to hyper-focus on an area. Once you feel you have mastered the sprint sessions, link several together (with breaks in between) to build up to marathon sessions — if that works for you. Finally, consider enlisting the help of a friend or relative to keep you accountable and give you honest feedback when you need it.

The first time you declutter, you most likely won't get rid of as much as you should. And keep in mind that decluttering is a repeated process that's like a revolving door — stuff comes in, and stuff goes out. When the revolving door becomes a one-way door that only allows stuff in and not out, then problems quickly arise. Items have life cycles and can only be used so much before breaking. Some items are used for seasons before they need to be passed on to the next person. It's easier to do when you begin to understand that decluttering is not just a one-time activity but rather — after the first big round of it — just a regular, more manageable upkeep. Think of it like moving into a home where the previous owners were not very clean. The first time, it took hours to clean, and everything from the windows to the ceiling to the baseboards had to be scrubbed down. After the initial cleaning, though, with a little bit of upkeep each week, you can get the whole house cleaned in a few hours. Decluttering won't take a few hours every week but will consist of just one chore per day that you can whip through in ten or fifteen minutes.

My friend Abigail struggles with procrastinating. When she actually begins a job, she does it quickly and efficiently — the biggest challenge for her is starting. There is always something else that needs to be done first, a project that needs more research before beginning, or a fear of making a mistake in the process. In a very real sense, it's an offshoot of perfectionism. For other people, procrastinating is the result of not scheduling a time to begin or feeling overwhelmed by the process. The more stuff people have, the more likely they will be afraid to start and be confronted with all the things they purchased over the years. Like the perfectionist, create a schedule and list and do your best to stick to it without being sidetracked by other chores.

The first step is often the most difficult. However, this is your home, and you've decided to declutter it. Show yourself that you can reach your goals and overcome even the most difficult of jobs. When you begin decluttering, you begin to pave your path to success.

Roadblocks are very common, and you should expect them. However, never let them stop you from achieving your dreams and goals. Use the exercises in this chapter to help you overcome them. The process is not a race or competition, so work at a pace that will ensure you ultimately complete the full declutter. You may have a unique circumstance preventing you from moving forward, but you can overcome the obstacle by using the frameworks discussed in this chapter.

KEY LESSONS FROM CHAPTER 7

- Everyone faces discouragements and roadblocks at times, but being aware of potential obstacles and challenges before they occur is the first step to overcoming them.
- Your mind is incredibly powerful and can feed you thoughts of doubt and worry. However, that same brain can reframe those thoughts into productive ones that result in action.
- Face underlying challenges as you encounter them, and learn to recognize what those may be for you so you can manage them better as you charge along in your home decluttering adventure.

CHAPTER 8:

Engaging Others in Your Plan and Getting Help

"Asking for help isn't giving up. It's refusing to give up."

– Amy Poehler

Most women face a constant struggle: do it yourself so you know it's done right, or ask others to help you and train them along the way to ensure future success. What to do? I think taking the time and asking others to help you is always worth the extra hassle. While it may be frustrating, particularly when people aren't jumping at the opportunity to help, a home includes everyone who lives there.

Throughout this chapter, we will discuss how to involve all household members and how to ask for external support when it comes to decluttering. You'll likely face some resistance (especially from kids), but involving others will change your home in the long term. When your kids and your partner realize how much work goes into maintaining a tidy and clean place, they will become more appreciative. You will be teaching your kids valuable lessons they can carry with them for the rest of their lives. There may even be a day when they thank you for it!

The Big Discussion

Telling family members that there is a new chore on the horizon is not always the most pleasant of conversations — especially when a partner or spouse isn't on board with the idea. While it may be a big discussion, treat it more as an activity to do together. For example, announce the decluttering activity over dinner rather than as a sit-down formal meeting to lay down the purpose and the ground rules.

Before you begin, make sure that the atmosphere is right. If your child just spilled their milk and is upset, if someone's angry about having to eat their broccoli, or if your spouse had a tough day at work, then it's best to wait a day until everyone is in a better mood.

When you broach the subject, take a respectful, calm approach to communicate with your family or roommate(s). Begin the conversation by explaining what you want to accomplish and why before sharing your vision of how your home and lives will improve when you all work together to declutter and change your habits to maintain a less cluttered home. Sharing your *why* can be a powerful way to help them better understand where you're coming from.

If you have children, ask them to share their ideas along with your partner or roommate(s). You may not realize it, but it's possible that they'll also get excited or motivated by the concept of transforming your home environment together. Let them contribute to the vision of a cleaner home and take charge of their rooms and play areas (under your supervision, of course). Incorporating a little input from others can help you get buy-in and cooperation.

If you encounter resistance to the idea, be patient. This is not a time to be angry or get worked up. Instead, focus on clear communication, ultimately having a productive conversation that results in decluttering action. Don't spread blame about whose fault the clutter is, and don't play the martyr and try to put all the blame on yourself either because that might make others resent you.

The first conversation should focus on getting buy-in unless you sense an appetite for more details. You don't want to overwhelm them with a big plan. Aim for understanding and general agreement first. Set the tone by communicating clearly and respectfully — no nagging, whining, yelling, or complaining. Good communication builds up and unites everyone. It embraces common values and teaches everyone that a decluttered home has benefits such as improved family time, more fun, less stress, and better health (and hygiene). That last one may not be a key reason kids want to get involved, but having better family time and more fun will get their attention. Later on, likely in a separate conversation, you can talk about specific plans, roles and responsibilities, and rewards to get everyone on the same page and working toward a common goal. Even if you know your plan when you have your first conversation, throwing everything at them all at once may be too much. The plan will likely be better received if you give them a little time to absorb what's coming their way.

Every project needs a leader, and you are the appointed leader for this project. Sometimes leaders do the work as well as delegates; in this case, you will most likely do most of the work. Areas such as the living room, kitchen, and bathroom will most likely fall to you, but play areas, garages, and bedrooms can easily be delegated to those using those areas. Personal belongings should always be decluttered by whoever owns them.

Part of your role as leader is to encourage others and ask them how you can support them in their appointed areas while also asking them to support you on this journey. Look at your leadership role as an opportunity to continue teaching and enforcing the concept of cleaning up when kids are done with what they're playing with or working on. Let this be positive reinforcement for them.

General Guidelines for Involving Children

Every child has different strengths, challenges, and abilities. Their capabilities are best known by their parents and the adults around them, so use your judgment about how much they can handle in a situation and day. A child in second grade isn't expected to write a thesis, nor should they be expected to declutter like you can. As they get older, you can build on the skills they've previously attained until they can complete the job independently with limited supervision.

Young children and toddlers don't have the same reasoning abilities you and I have. But don't underestimate their abilities. In fact, they may be better at it than you expect because they know what they play with and like, and might be able to grasp the concept of giving away an unwanted toy for other children to love (in adult terms, we call that donating). And if this is a stretch, at a minimum, teach and enforce the concept of cleanup after playtime.

Preschool (ages 3 to 4): For young children, ask them to pick a few toys they no longer play with or want and put them in the donate bin. While a child this age probably cannot grasp the concept of donating, make it more concrete for them by explaining that you are giving the unwanted toys to other children who don't have any. Basically, make it relatable and understandable to them. You can repeat the same process with clothing and trinkets. Ultimately, you will do the work, and they can help with some cleaning and putting the toys back in the right place. At this stage, you're showing them what needs to be done and asking them to join in and take some responsibility.

CHAPTER 8:

While some people think that you should go through this entire process with each one of the child's belongings, I don't do that. It's up to you, of course, but many children haven't developed their reasoning skills around this quite yet. I think it's great to get them involved to help a bit, learn the concept and value of what you're doing, and do a little sorting and letting go. That said, I'm all for doing the heavy decluttering when they're asleep or at school so you can make the progress you need to. Try to keep in mind things you know they love and want to keep, but feel free to get rid of all of the old party favors that add clutter, things they never play with and probably won't ever play with, and clothes that don't fit anymore. You get the picture.

Elementary School (ages 5 to 11): At this age, you teach children as they work alongside you. In many cases, you should be able to instruct them on a task-by-task basis and allow them to do the actual work.

Kids who are very independent and exhibit good decision-making skills can sometimes take care of most of the process so long as you check on them sporadically and after they're done sorting. You'll probably need to make a few adjustments and patiently answer any questions they have. When my eleven-year-old daughter did this, she did a fantastic job overall. She cleared out so much clutter that she unknowingly threw out gift cards and cash in the process. So be sure to check their work when they are done.

Middle School (ages 11 to 14): Middle school is a funny age, as kids sometimes still need a lot of help — or very little. You know your children best, so treat them as young teenagers but give them the guidance they need without talking down to them. For some, this may involve very basic instructions and step-by-step details, but other middle schoolers will need minimal direction.

High School and older: High schoolers are capable and should be able to declutter their environment effectively and independently. Share with them the process and key tips (such as the cheat sheets given in chapter five) on how to declutter. Remember that everyone has their strengths and challenges, but there's nothing like learning early and through repetition. When it comes to important documents like school applications, report cards, or anything financial, be sure to assist them because you don't want them to get rid of documents and books they may need later.

Working Together

Working together can be challenging but also very rewarding. As you lead those in your home through decluttering, remember to remain calm and communicate clearly. Express your feelings, but don't blame other people for the mess. Instead, extend your appreciation for other people's help by thanking and rewarding them for a job well done at the end of the day. If you're doing a full home declutter, you can think of a family reward, such as a trip to the beach or an amusement park. The rewards don't have to be expensive — they can simply reinforce that decluttering will improve family time.

One more tip. As you work with your family, be mindful not to micromanage or be too critical, as this will demotivate them (and then you'll ultimately end up doing it yourself!). If things need fine-tuning or tweaking, make the suggestions casually or when they're done. Hopefully, the kindness will be returned without too much complaining — after all, chores are not children's favorite thing to do! Cooperation is a good step in the right direction.

CHAPTER 8:

DO	DON'T
Stay calm and communicate clearly	Blame others for the mess
	Nag, yell, or shame others
Provide direction, coaching, and examples as needed	Criticize others who are helping for not meeting your exact expectations
Let go of a little control in exchange for a lot of help	
Respectfully express your feelings	Take over the job from someone helping you because you jump to the conclusion you can do it better
Show genuine appreciation and thank anyone who helps you	
Promptly reward and celebrate	

Resistance from Your Partner or Spouse

At the start of the chapter, we hinted that there may be some resistance from your spouse. So, what do you do when a loved one won't collaborate with you on this? Relationships and interpersonal dynamics are intricate and, unfortunately, beyond the scope of this book. Rather than hounding them, set up systems that can allow a transition to keeping your home decluttered. Above all, don't nag, and don't ruin the relationship over it.

Possible systems could include:
- Add a wastebasket in every room for garbage and arrange for it to be cleared out weekly.
- Ask for laundry and dishes to be put away daily.
- Ask your spouse if they would like to work together with you to declutter an area. If they say no, ask for permission to declutter their personal belongings.
- Start small — perhaps a sock drawer or junk drawer — and work your way up from there until you get stronger resistance.

- Be appreciative and always thank your spouse for all they do and the effort they are making.

Hiring a Professional

Every once in a while, there are jobs you just can't do. When a pipe gets clogged, you call a plumber. If termites infest your home, you call an exterminator. And sometimes, if the clutter has gotten out of hand, and you can't bear the thought of going through it yourself, you hire a professional.

Plenty of professional organizers thrive when dealing with other people's stuff. Other people, like nonjudgmental friends or coworkers who can be honest and keep you on track, may be great to ask for a helping hand and advice. Other options would be an online organizing group (Facebook groups or Reddit) and life coaches specializing in decluttering and organizing. Let's look further into how these different categories of people can help you become clutter-free.

Hiring a Helper or Professional Organizer

Let's be honest, hiring professionals can be expensive — and the more stuff you have, the more expensive it will be. Hiring a professional does not mean you're off the hook. You must remain a part of the process from start to finish, or you'll end up with missing items and an inadequate organizational system that just doesn't work for you.

Perhaps you don't need the entire job to be done by a professional organizer but need help with only one stage or room. You could find someone to come for a day to help you get started. Or you could hire someone less qualified but equally eager, such as a local high school or college student. A babysitter or housekeeper who has a few spare hours may also be willing to help.

Friends or Family

Many people love decluttering and organizing. I'm sure you can think of a few friends or family members who have super-organized (and clean) homes, love to drop "tips" about home improvement, and get great satisfaction from helping others and do it with ease. While their "help" may sometimes be frustrating, they are the ones you need in times like this.

There is also always the friend or family member asking if they can help you with anything — this would be an excellent opportunity to take them up on their offer. Likewise, ask anyone you think may be a good fit to work with you on this. You can always ask to pay friends or family for their time — or at the very least make them dinner — so that it's a mutually beneficial exchange. Another alternative is to ask (or pay!) your children to join you. With practice, my daughter became very good at decluttering and organizing when she was just twelve. In time, I began to pay her for her help when I struggled through difficult areas or just needed a fresh perspective. Compensating her for her work motivated and benefited both of us equally.

Online Groups

Online groups can be a great help. They can be ruthless in their feedback but equally encouraging. Online groups have the added benefit that most of the people in them have gone through decluttering, so they know exactly what you are going through. They can offer support and the accountability you need to stick to the task.

Moving Forward

Enlisting help — whether it be your family or professional help — will help you declutter and keep your home clutter-free for years to come. Don't be afraid to ask for assistance, as most people are more than willing to lend a hand.

KEY LESSONS FROM CHAPTER 8

- Focus on clear, respectful communication when broaching the subject of household decluttering, and work through resistance to find solutions for all parties involved.
- Kids are more than capable of decluttering and organizing, so let them help you. It will teach them lifelong lessons and lighten your load.
- Get creative about enlisting help, including hiring others to help you, even if it's for short stints of work to get you through the tough spots.

CHAPTER 9:

Organizing Systems That Work

"You can't reach for anything new if your hands are still full of yesterday's junk."

— Louise Smith

You've sorted and cleaned, and now it's time to organize (or reorganize) the stuff you've chosen to keep. While the primary focus of this book is not about organizing, it's worthwhile to address the subject because you'll most likely want to arrange the contents of your home to avoid falling into the clutter trap again. If you don't like organizing and putting things away, this is your chance to go through all the contents in your sorting area again and get rid of a few more things before you start! The fewer possessions you have, the less you need to organize. As Marie Kondo says, "Don't organize what you can discard."

Organizing your home will help to keep things running smoothly after you spent all that time decluttering. You'll have a home for each item when you set up organizational systems. This will help you put things away in the long term rather than allowing random things to pile up in random areas. When we get excited about something, one of the easiest ways to express it is to drop a few dollars on related products. But when organizing, avoid buying containers, boxes, and storage items until after decluttering. If you're like me, this is a tough one. I once had to force myself out of The Container Store without making a purchase during a big sale because I knew I had to purge my pantry before I started buying those gorgeous organizing bins and labels! I may have missed that sale, but my decision to walk out that day saved me money in the long run. Once you've sorted through your belongings, it will be easier to see what storage containers and sorting tools you'll need to keep them from becoming an unsorted mess again.

Organizational Tools

Large totes: Large items and long-term storage items (such as seasonal clothing and decorations) can all be stored in totes and bins. If buying them new, make sure they're clear so you can easily identify their contents.

Small and medium containers and baskets: From small items to groups of similar items, this size container can help keep things from getting lost in drawers and on shelves.

Dividers: Large drawers can be difficult to keep organized; however, adding in a few dividers will make it much easier to keep them tidy.

Hooks: Having enough hooks will help keep clothes and bags off the floor. The entryway, bathroom, and bedrooms are great places to add a few hooks.

Racks: From wire shelving units to spice and dish racks, racks are helpful in the kitchen to keep items of a similar nature together.

CHAPTER 9:

Cabinets, buffets, and armoires: No doubt these are larger pieces of furniture, but they can be very useful to create extra storage areas and serve as stylish additions to your space.

Organizational Principles

Principle #1: Sort Like with Like

Similar items should be gathered together because it helps identify what you have and gives a cohesive look.

Principle #2: Use Clear Bins

Clear bins allow you to see what's in them, which can prevent items from getting lost and forgotten. This will also help you save money whenever you don't have to buy something you already have. Labeling boxes is always helpful and will take your organization to the next level.

Principle #3: Don't Overcrowd an Area

When areas get too crowded, things get pushed to the back (or the bottom) of a shelf. This also includes keeping spaces around your storage area uncluttered and unobstructed. If you can't easily get to the shelf or cabinet where something is stored, you're much less likely to keep up with the organization and more likely to place things in areas where they don't belong instead of where they should go.

Principle #4: Sort and Store by Frequent Use

If you use an item frequently, put the items or organizational bins in an area close by and within easy reach. Seasonal items or items used less frequently can be put toward the back or in storage areas.

Principle #5: Establish Definitive Spaces

Group content together in set areas. Kitchen supplies belong only in the kitchen, and overflow items (such as small appliances) should be stored in the kitchen or adjacent areas, not in distant hall closets or bedrooms. Just like we have boundaries in many aspects of our lives, so does your stuff.

Organizational Hacks by Room

Bathroom: Under the sink is a great place to store extra toilet paper, toothbrushes, and soap. If your bathroom doesn't have a vanity cabinet, you can install an over-the-toilet cabinet, a mirror medicine cabinet, or a storage cabinet — a quick Google search will produce many useful cabinets that can fit any space.

Have a place where a few "like" products, such as towels and linens, can be stored. Stylish baskets can house these items on open shelving. You can also add an over-the-door rack to hang towels and bathrobes.

And don't forget about the shower! Adding a metal or plastic hanging caddy can give you space to store soaps, razors, and brushes. You can also add an extra shower bucket for bath toys (make sure it has plenty of holes so the contents can drain and dry easily).

Closets: Logic is your best friend when it comes to closets, and part of that is sorting similar items together. This could be grouping all the linens and towels together or putting clothes together by type, occasion, and color.

CHAPTER 9:

Speaking of clothing, let's take a few minutes to discuss this. Clothes need to be grouped together so that they don't get lost in the sea of garments. Dresses should be hung together in one area. Skirts and pants both have their areas as well. From there, long-sleeved shirts, dress shirts, and short-sleeved shirts can all hang together. Once organized by category, organize them by color, beginning with black, gray, brown, tan, then white, and then the order of the rainbow: red, orange, yellow, green, blue, indigo, and violet.

T-shirts and other types of tops that don't need to be hung can be folded and then stacked on their side to easily discern what you have available. First, organize tank tops, then short-sleeves, and finally long-sleeves. Then, sort it all by color.

Pants and shorts follow the same routine: separate them by joggers and sweats, leggings, long pants, jeans, and shorts. You can repeat the same for casual skirts that don't hang up.

If you don't have a chest of drawers, consider adding bins, dividers, or hanging organizers and shelves to your closet to keep things neatly sorted. Bins are also useful for sorting underwear, bras, socks, and pajamas. Hanging shelves can be great for T-shirts, workout clothes, scarves, accessories, and bed sheets.

Kitchen: Dividers and containers will be your best friend in the kitchen. There are dozens of kitchen organization solutions, so here is a brief list highlighting some of my favorites:
- Rectangular spice racks that can be fastened to the wall
- Magnetic knife holder
- Portable kitchen island
- Open shelving
- Pot rack over the kitchen island to create cupboard space
- Wooden or bamboo dividers added to large drawers to sort baking sheets, platters, and casserole dishes

- Reshelve the pantry and shrink a few areas to add in an extra shelf. Add glide-out shelves to cupboards and create sublevels for easy access and visualization.

Living Room: Perhaps one of the most well-used rooms in the house, the living room, should be a peaceful place. Having designated furniture for books, toys, blankets, and functional objects like TV remotes can help to keep it organized. Organize books by author or subject, or by color if you're just going for an aesthetic look, and toys by type and hide them away in neat bins. If you struggle with space, look for furniture with storage capabilities, like ottomans, coffee tables with drawers, and cabinets and bookshelves that have some closed cupboards.

Organizational Tips and Tricks

Every home has the infamous junk drawer filled with all sorts of miscellaneous items you just don't know how to sort. Adding dividers or small trays can help divide the space into manageable sections to keep it organized. Declutter this drawer once a month, and *never* extend it to two drawers. If it's overflowing, then it's time to declutter it again.

Each home should have at least one sentimental or memory box for each person. Let this box be personal, and even if other people think it's "junk," if it's in the box, it stays until the owner decides otherwise. The key to making these boxes successful is making them small — and only one per person. The specific size will depend on how much storage space you have in your home and how many people have to share the space, so you will have to use your own judgment.

CHAPTER 9:

Consider adding dividers, spacers, or boxes if things look messy in storage areas. Storage containers now come in all shapes and sizes, including long, thin boxes that fit under the bed or staircases. They can also be stacked vertically. Stackable containers are also helpful for storage areas, and shelving can be added to the basement, garage, and attic to make organization easier. A tip to keep things looking orderly is to use the same color storage containers throughout the area. That will provide a more uniform look, which will ultimately appear neater.

As you pull items from storage, rotate them so that the next season is always readily available. Since some seasons require more equipment, such as winter clothing and heavy blankets, vacuum bags can compress the space they take.

My final piece of advice is to make the most of your space, including vertical space like doors. This is especially important if you have limited space in your home. The backside of a door is a great place to hang peg boards, shoe organizers (which can hold much more than shoes), and towel hangers. If you actually have plenty of space in your home, you may not need to get creative with storage, and you're better off not doing this because it will only encourage you to hold onto more than you need in your home, which will catch up to you eventually. In other words, don't let the luxury of space enable a habit of holding onto more than what's loved and necessary.

Happy organizing!

KEY LESSONS FROM CHAPTER 9

- Avoid buying organizational supplies and tools until after you finish decluttering.
- Organize items by category before subdividing them into smaller areas. As a general rule, don't spread the same items to multiple places unless you have a legitimate functional reason for duplicates in different places.
- Utilize every space in your home and be creative with how to store items, especially if you are space-constrained.

CHAPTER 10:

Maintaining Long-Term Success

*"Success is the product of daily habits —
not once-in-a-lifetime transformations."*

– JAMES CLEAR

Decluttering your home is a big job, but you've done it area by area, so it was a manageable task that produced a well-ordered, tidy home. As much as you enjoyed the process (or perhaps you didn't), it's not a task that you want to tackle on a large scale every month. The question then remains, how do I stay clutter-free over the long haul?

Maintaining a neat, decluttered home must become a habit. Consistency will be your friend. Establishing a routine, habits, and a regular evaluation of all your belongings will help you stay on top of the mess and keep it at a manageable level. Depending on the size of your home, how likely you are to fall into clutter traps, and how many people live with you, you'll need to come up with a daily or weekly decluttering plan. Spending just ten or fifteen minutes a day doing upkeep may be all you need to do to make a big difference.

I made it a habit to spend about fifteen minutes daily tidying up. This includes putting things away, straightening up, and a bit of touch-up cleaning. To maximize my chance for success in maintaining these habits, I found times that fit into my schedule and are connected to other daily activities and habits. This is called habit stacking and is a method that works in many facets of life to create new habits. For me, I attach my daily decluttering time to things I do regularly — the morning right after I drop my girls off at school or the end of the day right before I make dinner. Having a schedule is the key to consistency. I like to focus on one area per day. For example:

Monday	Kitchen and dining room	Straighten the pantry, clear countertops and table space, go through the refrigerator
Tuesday	Living room	Straighten bookshelves, toy bins, coffee table
Wednesday	Bathrooms	Straighten bins, restock supplies, spot clean, pick up laundry
Thursday	Bedrooms	Clean up items left on the floor, straighten closets, clear excess items from dressers and side tables
Friday	Entryway and office	Clean up small items that get left around, straighten baskets and bins, clear spaces
Saturday	Paperwork	Go through the mail, pay bills, file receipts

Every month, these areas get an extra declutter, and it's enough to keep on top of it. When seasons change, I spend an extra hour or two to switch out the clothes and bedding and do a deeper purge of what I won't be keeping for the next time that season occurs.

Spaces like the garage, attic, and basement can be decluttered less often unless they are high-traffic areas that accumulate items frequently. Set a frequency that works for your schedule to declutter these areas and add it to your calendars. This could be quarterly or semi-annually.

All in all, find a consistent and maintainable time of day that works for your schedule. As you think about when you can fit time for this new habit into your life, consider stacking it onto something you already do daily. Established habits that you can consider attaching ten minutes of decluttering time before or after could include bringing in the mail, having your morning coffee, your workout, dropping off or picking your children up from school or an activity, eating lunch, or brushing your teeth. This will help maximize your success.

Remember, the key to developing a habit is starting. Don't overthink it. Choose your day to start, engage in the activity you want to do regularly, and that will be the start to changing your ways. Repeat it the next day and the day after that. With commitment, one day of spending ten minutes putting things away and straightening up will then turn into a week, then a month, and eventually a new way of life. If you need a little extra push as you build your new habits, you can create a simple tracker like a checklist or a sticker chart — who said we're too old for a sticker chart? There are also plenty of great habit tracker apps you can tap into.

Control What Comes In

The easiest way to maintain a decluttered home is to control what comes in. Every item you purchase, every sample you pick up, and every gift you receive is an item that comes into your home. If you don't begin to control what comes in, you'll be working against yourself for the rest of your life. The clutter will continue to build up and repeatedly get out of hand, and you'll be doing a full house decluttering on a regular basis or, sadly, succumb to a life of clutter.

Perhaps the biggest way to control what comes in is to watch what you spend money on. It's easy to fall for sales and good discounts, but always ask yourself if you would still buy the item if it wasn't on sale (unless, of course, it's something you've been waiting to go on sale for a while). Amazon Prime and all the other online retailers have made it very easy to shop online, and the constant availability and free shipping are a snare for many people.

Before buying something new, ask yourself if there isn't something you can use that you already own. Do you need another curling iron that is slightly larger? Do you need a new black top that has a slightly different cut than the four other black tops you already own? Many people think they *need* new items, but once you get in the mindset of using what you own, you build contentment and save money, along with saving your home from clutter.

Here are a few tips on controlling what comes into your home:
- Avoid samples and freebies. What are you going to do with a tenth of a product? Not much, and just like hotel shampoo and conditioner, they often go unused and are environmentally wasteful.
- Avoid small item purchases that are made just for the dopamine hit.
- Consider renting things such as snow equipment, home improvement tools, and special occasion dresses.
- Decline party favors or conveniently leave without taking one.
- Focus on purchasing quality items that can be used repeatedly.

Ultimately, aim for less clutter and not perfection. As time goes on, you will develop an eagle eye for items that turn into clutter, and it will become much easier to avoid purchasing them and to dispose of them when they're no longer needed. You'll

CHAPTER 10:

also be able to stop yourself from buying items that become clutter — after you've discarded the same item multiple times, it becomes quite obvious that you don't need to buy it again!

However, don't let all tidying and decluttering fall on your shoulders. Encourage family members and roommates to help you control the clutter and appreciate their efforts when they do. Speak with them about what you're doing, ask for their advice, and urge them to work with you on this new way of living.

Be mindful of the benefits you experience when you get rid of the stuff you don't need and get your clutter under control. Recognize the satisfaction you get from living in this reality compared to the negative feelings you harbored when your home was a mess. This will also fuel your motivation to uphold your new and improved lifestyle and reap the rewards.

My final piece of advice is to celebrate your progress and enjoy all that comes with a tidier home. You have come so far! You're changing your outlook on life and your future path. When setbacks occur, accept them, be compassionate with yourself, and keep moving forward to get and keep your home decluttered for good.

KEY LESSONS FROM CHAPTER 10

- Keep your home decluttered by implementing daily habits, working one day at a time.
- Create and implement a decluttering and tidying up schedule.
- Leverage habit-stacking tactics as you create new habits that will help you maintain a less cluttered home.
- Be mindful of every item that you allow in your home and become aware of tactics that encourage you to buy things you don't need.

Conclusion

*"If you own this story you get
to write the ending."*

– Brené Brown

The mess is gone. Your home is free of clutter, and a new lease on life has been given to you. You have taken the time to declutter, clean, and organize your home, and now you get to reap the benefits of all your labors. In the coming weeks and months, you'll begin to notice the lasting, transformative effects decluttering has on your life.

If you haven't been decluttering throughout the book, now is the time to begin and experience the impact of your efforts. Yes, it takes effort. Yes, it sounds like a really huge chore. But your life will be so much better because of it.

Decluttering your home is so much more than a chore. It's an act of self-care with the potential to transform your life in ways you might not even realize until you see or feel them. When you are drowning in stuff, you have neither the space nor the time for other people or things to enter your life, your mind, or your heart. What you might be missing or inadvertently blocking is the stuff that matters most. Those "things," people, or even clear thoughts may be more meaningful than you could ever imagine. By physically decluttering your home, you may feel like you're letting go of so much, and that can be scary and emotional. However, the space that you gain as a result can lighten your step, open up possibilities, free your mind and your spirit, and enable you to live your life in the present and for the future. You may come to realize that the old stack of magazines you've held onto is not what matters, but rather everything else that blossoms when you choose to let go of what you've saved for so long.

Establish your *why*, create a schedule, and begin the process of decluttering. Have fun along the way through all the milestones that bring you joy, whether that's having a yard sale, making a big donation to your favorite charity, or just watching your home open up with space as bags and boxes of stuff exit. Involve your family and let them be part of the process, reward yourselves, and celebrate — it will change their lives as much as it will yours.

Decluttering done successfully is an ongoing journey as seasons and lifestyles change. There are many resources and tools to help you along the way, and if you ever get stuck, just open this book once again and jump to the chapter that addresses the issue.

You have started a new journey, and it is life-changing. Now it's time to keep your wheels in motion and experience the greatness that can unfold.

Did you like the book? I'd love to hear your thoughts! Reviews are very helpful for independent authors like me, and I'd really appreciate it if you left a review on Amazon. I read every single one. Even if you don't have time to write a review, please click this QR code and leave a star rating!

Bibliography

Closet Factory. 'UCLA Study Finds Stress Caused by Clutter'. Closet Factory, 11 September 2017. https://www.closetfactory.com/blog/ucla-study-finds-stress-caused-by-clutter/.

David, Sam. 'Fascinating Statistics On Procrastination (Based On Research and Surveys)'. *Proactivity Lab* (blog), 3 January 2023. https://proactivitylab.com/fascinating-statistics-on-procrastination-based-on-research-and-surveys/.

Gaspar, John M., Gregory J. Christie, David J. Prime, Pierre Jolicœur, and John J. McDonald. 'Inability to Suppress Salient Distractors Predicts Low Visual Working Memory Capacity'. *Proceedings of the National Academy of Sciences* 113, no. 13 (29 March 2016): 3693–98. https://doi.org/10.1073/pnas.1523471113.

Raines, Amanda M., Joseph W. Boffa, Nicholas P. Allan, Nicole A. Short, and Norman B. Schmidt. 'Hoarding and Eating Pathology: The Mediating Role of Emotion Regulation'. *Comprehensive Psychiatry* 57 (February 2015): 29–35. https://doi.org/10.1016/j.comppsych.2014.11.005.

Roster, Catherine A., Joseph R. Ferrari, and M. Peter Jurkat. 'The Dark Side of Home: Assessing Possession "Clutter" on Subjective Well-Being'. *Journal of Environmental Psychology* 46 (1 June 2016): 32–41. https://doi.org/10.1016/j.jenvp.2016.03.003.

Saxbe, Darby, and Rena L. Repetti. 'For Better or Worse? Coregulation of Couples' Cortisol Levels and Mood States'. *Journal of Personality and Social Psychology* 98, no. 1 (January 2010): 92–103. https://doi.org/10.1037/a0016959.

Singla, Veena. 'Not Just Dirt: Toxic Chemicals in Indoor Dust'. Issue Brief. NRDC, 14 September 2016. https://www.nrdc.org/resources/not-just-dirt-toxic-chemicals-indoor-dust.

Vardoulakis, Sotiris, Evanthia Giagloglou, Susanne Steinle, Alice Davis, Anne Sleeuwenhoek, Karen S. Galea, Ken Dixon, and Joanne O. Crawford. 'Indoor Exposure to Selected Air Pollutants in the Home Environment: A Systematic Review'. *International Journal of Environmental Research and Public Health* 17, no. 23 (December 2020): 8972. https://doi.org/10.3390/ijerph17238972.

Vartanian, Lenny R., Kristin M. Kernan, and Brian Wansink. 'Clutter, Chaos, and Overconsumption: The Role of Mind-Set in Stressful and Chaotic Food Environments'. *Environment and Behavior* 49, no. 2 (1 February 2017): 215–23. https://doi.org/10.1177/0013916516628178.

Made in the USA
Monee, IL
27 November 2024